Young Children and Worship

Young Children and Worship

Sonja M. Stewart
and
Jerome W. Berryman

Westminster/John Knox Press
Louisville, Kentucky

Scripture quotations from the Revised Standard Version of the Bible are copyrighted 1946, 1952, © 1971, 1973 by the Division of Christian Education of the National Council of the Churches of Christ in the U.S.A. and are used by permission.

Part I, The Worship Center Order, and sessions 1–3, 13, 22–24, 30, 32–38, and 42–43 were written by Sonja M. Stewart. Sessions 5–8, 10–12, 14–21, 25–29, 31, 39–41, and 44 were written by Jerome W. Berryman. Sessions 4 and 9 were written jointly.

We dedicate this book to
JACK STEWART
and
THEA BERRYMAN

First edition

Published by Westminster/John Knox
Louisville, Kentucky

PRINTED IN THE UNITED STATES OF AMERICA

9 8 7 6 5

Library of Congress Cataloging-in-Publication Data

Stewart, Sonja M., date–
   Young children and worship / Sonja M. Stewart and Jerome W.
Berryman. — 1st ed.
      p.   cm.
   ISBN 0-664-25040-8 (pbk.)

   1. Worship (Religious education) 2. Children's sermons.
I. Berryman, Jerome. II. Title.
BV1522.S74 1989
264'.0880543—dc19   88-17766
                                                  CIP

Contents

Preface   7

Acknowledgments   11

PART I: INTRODUCTION   13
  Worship   15
  Storytelling   24
  Response: Wonder and Art   30
  How the Church Measures Time   34
  Getting Started   43

PART II: GETTING READY TO BE WITH GOD   55
  1. Orientation to the Worship Center   57
  2. Talking to God   61
  3. Listening to God   66
  4. Listening to One of God's Stories: The Light 71
  WORSHIP CENTER ORDER   77

PART III: PRESENTATIONS
  5. The Good Shepherd   85
  6. The Good Shepherd and the Lost Sheep   90

Stories from the Old Testament
  7. Creation   92
  8. Noah   96
  9. Abram and Sarai   100
 10. Exodus   104
 11. The Ten Best Ways to Live   108
 12. The Ark and a Tent for God   112
 13. The Promised Land   117
 14. The Temple, a House for God   120
 15. Exile and Return   123

Stories for the Church Year: Advent and Christmas

16. How the Church Tells Time   126
17. The Prophets Show the Way to Bethlehem (Advent I)   130
18. Mary and Joseph Show the Way to Bethlehem (Advent II)   133
19. The Shepherds Show the Way to Bethlehem (Advent III)   136
20. The Magi Show the Way to Bethlehem (Advent IV)   139
21. Christmas—Meeting the Christ Child   143
22. The Boy Jesus in the Temple   147

Stories for the Church Year: Epiphany

23. Jesus Is Baptized   150
24. Jesus in the Wilderness   153
25. The Mustard Seed   156
26. The Leaven   159
27. The Great Pearl   162
28. The Sower   166
29. The Good Samaritan   169
30. The Great Banquet   173

Stories for the Church Year: Lent

31. Lenten Puzzle   176
32. Jesus and the Children   178
33. Jesus and Bartimaeus   180
34. Jesus and Zacchaeus   183
35. Jesus the King   186
36. Jesus' Last Passover   189

Stories for the Church Year: Easter

37. Jesus Is Risen: Appearance to Mary Magdalene   193
38. Jesus Is Risen: The Road to Emmaus   196
39. The Good Shepherd and the Wolf   199
40. The Good Shepherd and the Lord's Supper (I)   201
41. The Good Shepherd and the Lord's Supper (II)   204
42. Ascension   207
43. Pentecost   209

Stories for the Church Year: The Season After Pentecost

44. Baptism   212

PART IV: PATTERNS AND INSTRUCTIONS   215

Preface

This book began in May of 1985 when Professor Sonja Stewart and two of her students from Western Theological Seminary in Michigan came to Houston for a workshop at Christ Church Cathedral, where I am the Canon Educator. At that workshop I presented the approach to religious education I had been developing since 1972 and some of the empirical research and theory upon which it is based.

This led to conversation and an invitation to Western Seminary for a "Children and Worship" conference in the fall of 1986. We met in the seminary's new model worship center, which Dr. Stewart had set up as part of her "Children and Worship" project. My presentations involved lectures, demonstrations of how to present the lessons to children, and question-and-answer sessions. Dr. Stewart studied the conference video record and my articles and lesson plans as a part of her own research.

This book brings together our two perspectives. Dr. Stewart's contribution comes from her work in early childhood education, spiritual formation, Christian worship, and the function of symbols and religious imagination in Christian formation. Her many years as a professor of Christian education and a teacher of teachers have contributed to this collaboration in important ways. The focus of her perspective is on children and worship.

My approach comes from daily experience in the classroom and as the headmaster of a school, as well as continuing work in churches of all sizes. Perhaps, the most profound influence on my approach to this work was more than ten years in the Texas Medical Center. I was first a Fellow and then an Assistant Professor at the Institution of Religion and was an Adjunct Assistant Professor of Pediatric Pastoral Care at Baylor College of Medicine. In addition, my work in the hospitals and at Houston Child Guidance Center as part of the crisis team was of major importance.

My focus is on the function of religious language—parable, sacred story, and liturgical action—in the moral and spiritual development of children. I am especially interested in how this powerful language discloses a "world" where God is present to help cope with and transcend the existential issues—death, aloneness, the threat of freedom, the need for meaning—that box us in and define children and adults as human beings. This perspective naturally includes the experience of worship.

This book actually began for me in 1971–72 when our family lived in Bergamo, Italy. I was studying at the Center for Advanced Montessori Studies and had a vague idea of applying the Montessori method to religious education. What I discovered was that Maria Montessori (1870–1952) had already made that application. Sofia Cavalletti, a distinguished Hebrew scholar and author, came from Rome that winter to lecture, so I also had the opportunity to meet the world's leading expert on Montessori and religious education. She and I have worked together ever since. My gratitude to Dr. Cavalletti for her wisdom and friendship all these years is beyond words.

A lesson in this book called "How the Church Tells Time" (Session 16), can be traced back to Montessori. This is especially important to note, because the roots of the approach presented by this book go back through three generations of development.

The influence of Montessori is generally apparent in this approach to religious education, but Cavalletti's influence is more direct. Look especially at the lessons about the Good Shepherd (Sessions 40 and 41) to see examples of her patient and careful work with children. The material is somewhat reworked by Dr. Stewart's and my interpretations, but Cavalletti's important and elegant connection between the Good Shepherd and the Holy Eucharist is obvious, and its spirit is clearly there. Concerning this lesson Dr. Cavalletti once said to me, "Isn't it simple. It only took me and the children about fifteen years to develop it, and I needed Vatican II to open up its possibilities."

It has been my dream to have clusters of churches working with seminaries of various traditions as research and development centers in this and other countries. This is to keep the theological, biblical, and educational preparation for the lessons faithful, scholarly, and alive as well as to keep the training from becoming identified with a single tradition. Such cooperation between seminary and church could maintain ongoing empirical research and enhance the further development of appropriate lessons and materials. Such collaboration could also contribute to a more adequate understanding of child development. Professor Stewart and her colleagues have made this dream a reality at Western Theological Seminary. Training and research related to this approach are now formally included in Western's M.Div. and M.R.E. degree programs, as well as in workshops to train worship-education leaders.

Now the book is done! For over a decade worship leaders, teachers, scholars, parents, workshop participants, and others have been asking for it. The push and pull of parish realities did not allow much time for such a publication, so Dr. Stewart took the matter in hand and did something about it!

We have hesitated to publish these lessons because they are best introduced personally. As you know, oral communication is much different from that of the printed page, but these lessons needed to be in a more accessible form, both to aid workshop participants and to communicate this approach more widely to further assess how it can be used best. For more information about workshops, please write to Dr. Stewart at Western Theological Seminary, Holland, Michigan 49423 or to me at Christ Church Cathedral, 1117 Texas Avenue, Houston, Texas 77002.

There are many people to thank in addition to Dr. Cavalletti and Dr. Stewart. The children deserve our special gratitude, for they have taught us all. Their parents, too, deserve our thanks for sharing their children with us.

My deepest thanks go to Thea, my collaborator in this work as well as in life. She is a master teacher of music to children and a devoted child advocate. Much of my credibility with the children who come to our center on Saturdays from the school where Thea works is because I am "Mrs. Berryman's 'Mr. Berryman.'" As you might expect, most of this work goes on in what might be called family time. Instead of competing, however, it has become a family project. Our daughters, Alyda and Coleen, grew up with it, and now they both help in more ways than they know. I thank them for being, and for being such help.

JEROME W. BERRYMAN

Acknowledgments

This book was made possible through the contributions of many people who have assisted in innumerable ways. I am indebted to the many students and workshop participants whose insights and accounts of children's responses helped to refine the stories and materials.

Special thanks are due to my assistant, Helene Vander Werff, who has helped in ways too numerous to report. For her assistance with "Children and Worship" workshops, and her contributions to the research by testing this approach in various settings and with many ages, I am especially grateful.

This has been a family project. My son and daughter-in-law, Calvin and Tawnya Stewart, have assisted me significantly in teaching and research. Their young children, Olivia and Merrick, helped too. I am grateful for constant encouragement and help from my husband, John, and our sons Todd and Keith, who also transported shelves, sand, desert boxes, and countless materials to various places I have taught. And appreciation goes to my parents, Malcolm and Rachel Forgrave, who proofread the manuscript and searched the mountains of New Mexico for just the right "Mount Sinai" and "Mount of Temptation" stones for our worship center.

I am deeply grateful to my colleagues at Western Theological Seminary, particularly to President Marvin Hoff and Professor Robert Coughenour, formerly Dean for Academic Affairs, for believing in my vision and providing the children's worship center and other resources necessary to the project, and to Professor Donald Bruggink for his photographic work.

Special thanks go to Robert Penning, for designing figures for the parable presentations, and to Robert and Marilyn VanderVeen, for generously providing a quiet place on Lake Michigan for writing.

I express, for many, appreciation to Sofia Cavalletti for the idea of linking the Good Shepherd with the Eucharist, and Christ the Light with baptism, and for encouraging others to adapt this to their religious traditions.

And my deepest gratitude goes to Jerome Berryman for the collaboration that permitted the writing of this book.

Pentecost, 1988   SONJA M. STEWART

PART I

INTRODUCTION

This book is about worship and young children. It describes an exciting way these children experience God while learning about God. It involves helping children worship in a special place *apart* from the worshiping congregation so they become able to worship meaningfully *with* the congregation.

While we believe that young children should be included in Sunday worship, we are aware that most congregations dismiss them for part if not all of the service. If you are like us, you are concerned about what happens in that precious time. Our work in worship and the church year, spiritual formation, and the church's ministry with children led us to search for appropriate ways that children from three through seven years of age could experience and worship God.

What follows is a way of being in worship with young children. It is a way that both you and the children can grow in love for God and for one another. It uses a sensorimotor style of storytelling as a primary means for encountering God, so God is experienced, not just learned about. It gives appropriate freedom, so young children can respond to stories of God through continued working with the story figures and art materials. It enables young children to bring their lived experiences into dialogue with God in the biblical stories. And, remarkably, it provides a way for young children to tell the stories of God to others.

The key to this approach is a worship context for telling and working with biblical stories, instead of a school environment. There are three reasons for choosing a worship context.

First, the intent of worship is to experience and praise God. While the experience of God in worship leads to knowledge of God, the primary mode of knowing is by participation. God is experienced as we enter into scripture and allow the Holy Spirit to convince us of the truth of God's word.

Second, worship transforms ordinary time and space into sacred time and space. The experience of God is one of mystery, awe, and wonder. Where education attempts to explain and interpret mystery, worship allows us to experience and dwell in the presence of God as a way of knowing. The time and space of worship engage a special remembering, called "anamnesis." Anamnesis is a way of bringing both the Christian community's experiences of God from the past and God's promised future into our present experience through memory, imagination, and meaning. So when we hear God's word proclaimed in word and sacrament we find ourselves "participating" in the original event or experience. Together with Jesus' first disciples and all the others, right up to the present, we commune in the breaking of the bread. The experience of sacred time and space in a special place set aside for God enables us to experience God in every time and every place.

A third reason for choosing a worship context is that it meets the needs of the young child. Young children need God and a religious community. They need love, security, appropriate freedom, continuity, order, and meaning. The ritual of worship in the children's worship center meets these needs. In worship, God is central. We find meaning and order in relation to God. When all is said and done, life and death have meaning only in that we belong to God. The worship context described here allows children to bring their own experiences into dialogue with the biblical stories so the children themselves have a way of making meaning and order in their lives.

Children do love and worship God, but they need to be introduced to the meaning and actions of corporate worship in a sensorimotor way. They need to know how to find the quiet place within, which enables them to get ready to worship "all by themselves" rather than sit in church in an imposed silence. They need to experience the essential parts of worship freed from the details of corporate worship, but in a worshiping atmosphere instead of a class where worship is merely explained. Our goal is to create an environment that enables young children to encounter and worship God. Here they abide in God's love as experienced in biblical stories, parables, and liturgical presentations, in order to make meaning and order in their lives and, as the body of Christ, live as Christ's ministers in the world.

It is difficult to write about this approach because it is primarily visual, oral, and kinesthetic. It needs to be experienced. Writing a book on how to worship with children is like writing a book on how to dance or play football. How does one write about the wonder, the mystery, and the experience of the presence of God, which is so essential to telling the stories of God and leading children in worship? We begin, hoping the Spirit of God will trigger your imagination so you may experience what happens in children's worship centers. Perhaps a description of one of our sessions can provide a reference point. Journey with us to a small Colorado church. Let your imagination carry you into a special place to be with God, to hear the stories of God, and to talk with God.

Worship

Where two or three are gathered in my name, there am I in the midst of them.—Matthew 18:20

Tucked in among snowcapped mountains of Colorado is a little church where twelve young children and their worship leader meet each Sunday. They have turned a small room into a special place to be with God. Along each wall are low bookshelves. On those shelves are intriguing gold parable boxes and smooth wooden biblical figures waiting to come to life in the hands of young storytellers. There are crayons and markers, paints and paper, scissors and paste, all neatly arranged, each in its own place.

This Sunday, as every Sunday, the children and their worship leader are sitting on a taped circle on the floor in front of the shelves. They are beginning to shift from ordinary time and place to the special time and place of worship, a time and place where they sense the presence of God. "This is a very special place," their worship leader says. "This is a special place to be with God, to hear the stories of God, to listen and to talk with God. We need a way to get ready to be with God. You can get ready all by yourself." They sing "Be Still and Know That I Am God" to help them.

When they are ready, they watch closely as the worship leader walks toward a shelf. Which story will she get? they wonder. Ah. It's in a gold box.

Carefully placing the box on the floor in front of them, she says, "I wonder if this is a parable? Hmm. It might be. Parables are very precious, like gold, and this box is gold." She runs her hands gently over the box. "This looks like a present. Well, parables are like presents. They have already been given to us. We can't buy them, or take them, or steal them. They are already ours. There's another reason why this might be a parable. It has a lid. And sometimes parables seem to have lids on them. But when you lift the lid of a parable there is something very precious inside. I know. Let's take off the lid and see."

Placing the gold box to her side, she opens it a wee bit, so the children can't see inside, and takes something out: a large green felt circle. "This is so green," she says as she lays it down on the floor. She begins running her hands over it, smoothing it out. "It's so soft and warm. I wonder what could be so green? Perhaps it is a large green meadow." She removes other pieces of felt from the box and wonders about each as she places them on the green meadow. There is an oval-shaped light blue piece; it might be a pool of water. There are three pieces of dark blue felt; they could be dangerous rocky places. There are several strips of tan felt. They seem to make a very strong log cabin, but when five laminated-cardboard sheep are placed inside, it's clearly a sheepfold. Then she pauses and sits back a moment. Something very important is about to happen.

Concentrating deeply on the scene, she begins. "Once there was someone who said such amazing things and did such wonderful things that people began to follow him. But they didn't know who he was. So one day they simply had to ask him, and he said, 'I am the Good Shepherd.' " She takes the Good Shepherd, made of laminated cardboard, from the box and places it beside the sheepfold. "I know each one of my sheep by name." She gently touches each sheep. "And they know the sound of my voice."

Matching her words to her actions, she moves the Good Shepherd and the sheep across the meadow to the cool water, through the places of danger, and safely back to the sheepfold.

"I wonder if the sheep have names?" Several children give names and continue to express their wonder in a dialogue. "I wonder if the sheep are happy? . . . I wonder how many sheep really could live in this place? . . . I wonder how the sheep feel about the Good Shepherd . . . and how the Good Shepherd feels about the sheep? . . . I wonder if you have ever had to go through places of danger or were lost and someone found you? . . . I wonder where this place might really be? . . ."

When the wondering is finished, the worship leader says, "Watch closely how I put these materials away so they will be ready for the next person to use." Slowly and silently she puts the materials back in the parable box and places it in its place on the shelf. Then she returns to the circle and asks, "I wonder if you would like to make something that shows how you feel about this parable. Or perhaps there is some other work you'd like to do." One at a time, as she goes around the circle, they decide and go to get their work.

A five-year-old girl is working with the Good Shepherd materials. She adds a row of wooden blocks between the still water and the places of danger. "There. Now we have the paths of righteousness," she says. Then, saying the Twenty-third Psalm, she moves the Good Shepherd and the sheep through the green pasture, by the still water, and along the paths of righteousness.

Several children are drawing pictures of houses and sheepfolds as they reflect on the story. A seven-year-old has drawn a self-portrait. Wearing a bright purple dress, she is standing beside an A-frame house. "Today is my birthday," she explains. "This is Debbie's house. I'm staying here. I don't know how long. I don't know where my daddy is, or my brother." Her parents are very poor, and the children often have to stay with other families. Here in the security of the Good Shepherd parable, she works on this critical life issue.

When it is time to get ready for the "feast," the children put their work away and gather again on the circle to hear part of Psalm 23 read from the Bible, to present their offerings, and to pray. Then they make "tables" with paper napkins, and fruit, cheese, bread, and juice are served. When the feast is over and the cups and napkins collected, they sing until their parents come. As parents arrive, each child goes to the leader for a personal good word and a benediction.

THE FOURFOLD ORDER OF WORSHIP

Now that you have an idea of how we worship with young children, we can describe our approach more fully and present the stories we tell.

Our experience with young children convinces us that they know, love, and worship God. But corporate worship is structured and full of words and symbols based on stories and memories children do not yet have. For children to participate meaningfully in corporate worship, they must first experience the essential parts and stories of worship through sensorimotor means. Our children's worship centers permit this. In the worship centers the flow of activity corresponds to the order of congregational worship instead of the traditional sequencing of nursery schools.

In Christian worship, the scattered people of God come together to praise, listen, and respond to God by celebrating the creative and redemptive acts of God, particularly the resurrection of Christ. The order of the service helps us do this. Christian worship has a fourfold structure, regardless of denomination or tradition. Your service may be highly liturgical or informal, even spontaneous, but the fourfold order is there. This order reflects the ordinary social activities of family celebrations: gathering, listening, thanking, and going. Expressed in the language of worship, this weekly celebration of the family of families uses terms such as these to order the time together: "Assemble in God's name," "Proclaim God's word," "Give thanks to God" (Eucharist), and "Go in God's name," for example.

The first and fourth parts of the order are preparatory in the sense that the first helps us get ready to be with God in the word and sacrament, while the fourth helps us get ready to reenter the ordinary world to do Christ's ministry and mission. The two middle parts are sometimes called the Liturgy (or Service) of the Word and the Liturgy (or Service) of the Lord's Supper. Sometimes the terms are different. You might call these four "The Approach to God," "The Word of God in Proclamation," "The Word of God in Sacrament," and "The Response to God." Substitute your names if you wish. We have used the Presbyterian order here.

THE ORDER OF WORSHIP AND YOUNG CHILDREN

To work with young children, we focused on the foundational and essential components of worship and on the biblical stories that give content to the images, symbols, and actions of worship. We took each part of the order of worship, selected the most essential parts for young children, and developed our approach around these parts. What follows is a description of the four parts of the order of worship and what we chose to do with young children for each part.

1. Assemble in God's Name

Each Sunday as we gather around the Lord's Table (altar), the first part of the order of worship helps us move from the world of ordinary time and place to the holy.

> Call to Worship
> Hymn of Praise
> Confession
> Declaration of Pardon
> Response of Praise

As we gather we need a way to get ready to be with God, to move our attention from ourselves and our world to God. So our approach to God, our gathering in God's name, is a time for preparing ourselves to listen to God. While getting ready comes from within, the liturgy helps us refocus and center in God as it shifts our everyday language to religious or biblical language, images, symbols, and signs of God. We greet one another in the name of the Lord. We sing and speak our praise to God. We confess our sins so that our relationship with God is restored and nothing stands in our way of being ready to listen to God.

Two things are essential in the first part of the order for worship: our awareness of the presence of God and our ability to get ready to be with God.

Just as pastors and elders meet before the worship service for preparation and prayer, so the children's worship leader and the greeter (or greeters) arrive early. While the greeter prepares the "feast," the worship leader sits on the circle on the floor, praying and becoming centered in God in order to be ready when the first child arrives. The greeter moves to the door to meet the children. While still outside the room, each child begins to prepare to enter this special place to be with God.

The leader greets each child as he or she sits down on the circle. New children are introduced and conversation continues until all have arrived. Then the leader helps transform this ordinary time and place into a special time and place to be with God.

The Call to Worship

"This is a very special place," the leader says. "It is very special because God is here. In this place we have all the time we need. So we don't have to hurry. We can walk more slowly. And we talk more softly, because someone might be talking with God, and we don't want to disturb them. This is a special place to be with God, to talk with God, to listen to God, and to hear the stories of God. So we need a way to get ready to be in such a special place with God. You can get ready all by yourself. You don't need me to tell you to get ready. Quietness comes from inside you, not from someone telling you to be quiet. You can get quiet all by yourself."

The Greeting

When the children are ready, a formal liturgical greeting in the name of the Lord is exchanged. We use greetings that coincide with the seasons of the church year. But for the youngest children, perhaps two are enough. From September to Easter we say, "The Lord be with you," and the children reply, **"And also with you."** This greeting is used in various places in the liturgy and is the first part of the greeting exchanged at the beginning of the Great Prayer of Thanksgiving. From Easter to September we exchange the great resurrection affirmation. The leader says, "Christ is risen," and the children reply, **"The Lord is risen indeed."**

Songs of Praise

We sing one or two songs of praise such as "O God, We Adore You"* or "Praise God from Whom All Blessings Flow." We end by singing "Be Still and Know That I Am God" as a way to get ready to hear a story of God and to mark our transition to the second part of the order of worship. Your church organist or music director can help you find music.

2. Proclaim God's Word

The second part of worship involves hearing and responding to the word of God. It looks something like this.

> [Hearing the Word of God]
> Prayer of Illumination of the Holy Spirit
> Old Testament Lesson
> Psalm
> New Testament Lesson
> Sermon
> [Responding to the Word of God]
> Hymn or Creed
> Baptism, Commissioning or Confirmation, Reception of Members
> Prayers of Intercession
> Offering

When we are ready to listen to God's word proclaimed through scripture and sermon we want to receive it as God intends, so we ask the Holy Spirit

---

*This is our adaptation of the first verse of "Father, I Adore You" by Terrye Coelho. It and "Be Still and Know That I Am God" are in *Songs for Worship,* compiled by John Michael Talbot (Sparrow Birdwing Music, Chatsworth, California 91311).

to guide us as we hear and respond. After scripture is read, a sermon provides an interpretation of and witness to God's word today. But just listening to God's word is not enough; the word of God invites response. We respond to the word in a variety of ways: with a hymn, confession of faith, baptism, prayers, and offerings.

The actions of receiving and responding to God's word are the heart of worship in the children's center. For young children, one biblical or liturgical story each session is enough, and it needs to be told and responded to in ways appropriate to young children. As we have said, this requires a sensorimotor approach, using materials children can work with after the story is presented, and an environment of appropriate freedom in which they can repeat the story and incorporate it into their lives.

The parable of **The Good Shepherd and the Lost Sheep** illustrates our procedure. The storytelling and the response time are so important they are discussed in separate sections. For now, we will say that after the singing of "Be Still and Know That I Am God" the story begins as the leader walks to the shelf where the parable or story is kept. The materials are visual translations of the Bible and are treated as such. The leader returns to the circle and places the materials on the floor. In good biblical fashion, the story is told using as few words and materials as possible.

The response time follows the story and takes two forms: a time of wondering and reflecting together on the story and a time for personal response and continued working with the story and art materials. After the wondering, each child personally decides what "work" he or she will do. Since the orientation sessions have shown the children how to select a place to work and how to get their materials and put them away, they are now free to move about the room "all by themselves." In this way they can interact with the materials as the Spirit moves them.

To give closure to the response time the children return to the circle, where the story or parable of the day is read from the Bible. Having seen the story presented and having personally worked with it, they can now picture the story and bring memories to it as they hear it read, a skill they will carry into corporate worship. Their offerings are presented and the transition to the third part of the order of worship occurs.

3. Give Thanks to God (Eucharist)

Each Sunday is a feast day celebrating the resurrection of Jesus Christ, and we gather around Christ's table to be fed by him.

> Preparation of the Lord's Table
> Great Prayer of Thanksgiving
> The Lord's Prayer
> Words of Institution
> Breaking of Bread, Pouring of Wine
> The Communion

At this solemn but joyful feast, we offer our thanksgiving to God through the Great Prayer of Thanksgiving (the Eucharistic Prayer), which summarizes God's mighty acts, from creation to the promise of Christ's return. We thank God for creation, the covenant, the Law and the Prophets, and for Jesus Christ and the promise of Christ's return. Together we pray the Lord's Prayer. Then we listen to the words of institution and witness the taking, blessing, breaking, and giving of the bread and wine. United in one body, we commune together.

In most Protestant congregations the Lord's Supper is not celebrated weekly, but the Great Prayer of Thanksgiving and the Lord's Prayer are offered. Of course, the Lord's Supper is not celebrated in the children's worship centers. But indirect preparation for the Eucharist is. The atmosphere is one of joy, warmth, thanksgiving, and fellowship. The children offer their own prayers of thanksgiving, in place of the Great Prayer of Thanksgiving, by saying the last two lines of the exchange. The leader says, "Let us give thanks to the Lord our God," and the children reply, **"It is right to give thanks and praise."** (Later in the year, when the children have learned these words, add the two preceding lines of the exchange as follows: The leader says, "Lift up your hearts," and the children reply, **"We lift them up unto the Lord."** Then continue with the two lines they already know.)

A "feast" follows. The children prepare "tables" with their white napkins, and fruit, cheese, bread, and juice are served. This is a pleasant time of talking and sharing. Sometimes we talk about food and great feasts Jesus gave, such as the feeding of the five thousand, or about Messianic banquets.

4. Go in God's Name

When the feast is over and the cups and napkins collected, we move to the fourth part of the order of worship.

Hymn
Charge
Blessing
Going Into the World as Christ's Ministers

Just as the first part of the service is a time for getting ready to be with God, so the fourth part is a time for getting ready to go into the world as the body of Christ, living as Christ's ministers and missionaries. Having experienced God and being renewed by God's grace, we know that the God who is present in this special time and place can be present with us in every time and every place. We sing a hymn of praise and are commissioned to be a source of God's healing in the world. We are then told to go out into the world in peace, to render no one evil for evil, to love and serve the Lord. Finally, we receive the benediction as a sign of God's presence, the presence of the Holy Spirit empowering us for ministry and mission.

In the children's worship center we sing until the parents arrive. The greeter tells each child when his or her parent comes. Then the child goes to the leader and is hugged or touched and receives a good word said quietly, so no one else can hear. This word names a gift for ministry observed that day, such as "Your smile made me feel so good today" or "Thank you for helping serve the feast" or "The storybook you made for Jim will help him while he has to stay in the hospital." Then a benediction is given, ending with "Go in peace."*

SIGNING

In the worship center we use signing for the deaf instead of finger plays. Signing is another way we can talk to God and to each other. It is a concrete way to include deaf children and to learn from them.

The language of signing communicates meaning, imagination, and memory just as words do. It portrays feeling and stirs emotion. Its rhythm is appropriate to use with songs and greetings exchanged in the worship center. The signs can become meaningful worship gestures that are quieting and enable us to worship God with our whole being.

Children seem to value the experience of signing and often recall the

Easter Greeting

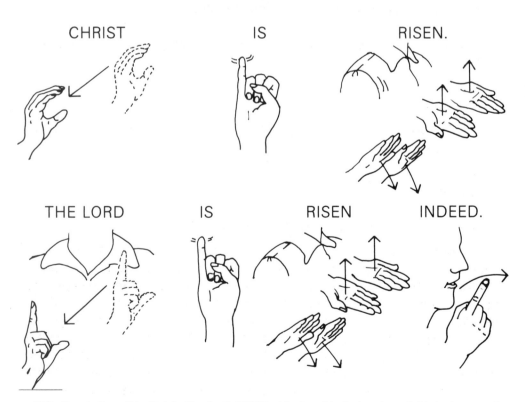

CHRIST   IS   RISEN.

THE LORD   IS   RISEN   INDEED.

*"Go Now in Peace" by Natalie Sleeth, © 1976 by Hinshaw Music, Inc., is available in sheet music.

signing more quickly than the words of a new song. As they learn to "read" the signs of songs and liturgical exchanges, they also learn to "read" the gestures and movement used in telling the biblical stories and consequently the gestures of the pastor or priest in worship, particularly as used in baptism and the Lord's Supper. The following resources may be helpful: *The Joy of Signing* and *Talk to the Deaf* by Lottie L. Riekehof; *Sign Language* by Louie J. Fant, Jr.; *Ministry to the Deaf* by Croft M. Pentz and Carter E. Bearden; and *Religious Signing* by Elaine Costello.

Storytelling

When a person has an experience of God there is a desire both to reexperience it and to tell it to others. But how do we communicate an experience with the invisible? We compose a story, and through that story we relive the experience as well as communicate it to others.

Storytelling also permits the listener to participate in the event and share in the experience of the storyteller. Such is the case with the stories, parables, and liturgical expressions of the Bible. They are our primary sources for experiencing and knowing God. These shared sacred memories of the people of God, told from generation to generation, continue to provide our knowledge of God, to form our identity as the people of God, and to give meaning to our acts of worship.

In educational settings the Bible is primarily used as a means of instruction. Some use it to teach morals, others theological concepts. In effect God is talked about, and the story's usefulness is over when the moral or theological concept is learned.

In worship, through the power of the Holy Spirit, God is made known to us in the hearing of the word. God is experienced and known as we enter into the story. We have said that this process of entering scripture involves remembrance, anamnesis. Through memory, imagination, and meaning, we bring to the text not only our personal experiences but also the shared experiences of the church through the ages. These stories, so sacred to the community, are not ones we put aside after a point is learned. Rather, they are told over and over again, from one generation to the next, constantly revealing new knowledge of God, deepening our faith, and recomposing our worlds. Our personal stories join with the community's sacred stories to tell us who we are and why we are here. They confer identity, meaning, and order.

Since in worship the story is a means by which the community meets God *together,* the function of the storyteller is not to instruct or entertain an audience of students, for there is no audience in worship. All are worshipers, and the storyteller wants to enter the story and disappear so that others may enter it also. The storyteller wants to get out of the way, so everyone can experience, praise, and listen to God. It is this shared experience of the holy that forms and unites the Christian community.

THE NATURE OF BIBLICAL NARRATIVE

Biblical narrative uses a particular technique that makes stories interesting and meaningful, to young children as well as to adults. Biblical stories tell only the actions and description essential to the story. The omission of definitions and unnecessary detail provides silences, time and space through which the listener experiences the mystery, awe, and wonder so characteristic of sacred story. This use of essential words and meaningful silences, and the omission of definitions and details, is unfortunately overlooked by most writers of biblically based stories for children. Because they do not understand the nature of biblical story and the function of anamnesis, they fill in the silences with descriptions and definitions, believing they are making the story more understandable. In so doing, they eliminate room for the imagination and the Holy Spirit to work and make the stories difficult to remember and, in some cases, to believe. Often even the response is prescribed, leaving no reason for personal and communal dialogue with God.

STORIES FOR CHILDREN'S WORSHIP

In wishing to honor and recapture a biblical way of storytelling, we have tried to discover the essential elements in the stories and tell them without embellishment. Staying close to the biblical text helps eliminate unnecessary words, while using materials to tell the story provides meaningful silences. For example, in the parable of **The Good Shepherd and the Lost Sheep,** we do not interrupt the story by naming the sheep as they are put in the sheepfold. They are placed in silence. Often silence has more power to attract and retain attention than words, for our minds fill it in. Further, the fact that sheep drink only from still water, and similar information, is irrelevant to the story. It is enough to say, "He shows them the way to the still water."

Choice of Stories

Our decision of which stories to tell young children was influenced by the nature of biblical stories. If the principle of telling the essential and omitting unnecessary description is applied to the choice of stories to be told to young children, it means that we tell first the stories most characteristic of our formation as the people of God. Stories that deepen and provide more information for the essential stories are told later. For example, the story of the exodus is foundational. Its major theme is that the people of God were slaves, and God led them through the waters to freedom. The children do not need to know the story of Moses' birth, how Moses left and returned to Egypt, or about the plagues, to understand the exodus. These stories deepen the essential exodus story and will be told later. The Old Testament stories that are foundational to the faith formation of the people of God and give meaning to our life and worship are the Creation, the Flood, the Exodus, the giving of the Law, the Ark of the Covenant, the Tabernacle, the Land, the Temple, and the Exile. Beginning with Advent we follow the themes of the church year, using the stories of Jesus' birth, visit to the Temple, baptism, and temptation, followed by parables and stories that represent Jesus' proclamation and signs of the kingdom of God. Jesus' death, resurrection, and ascension and the coming of the promised Holy Spirit at Pentecost are told during Lent and Easter. In this way the one story of God's creation and redemption in its most essential form is presented in sequence.

These stories continue to form and give meaning to the worship life of the Christian community, so we tell them from a worship perspective. They give a context and provide some of the words that are used in the liturgy, particularly in the sacraments of baptism and the Lord's Supper. In effect the children in early childhood hear the stories for which the congregation praises God in the Great Prayer of Thanksgiving. By the end of the year the children will have memories, imagination, and meaning to pray the great Eucharistic prayer with the worshiping congregation.

These stories also correspond to the needs of children and speak to their fears. Children have needs for love, security, growth, continuity, belonging, and caring for others and for the environment. They also need to create meaning and order in their lives, and particularly in facing in their fears. These stories of God speak to their fears of being abandoned, lost, or alone, of pain, suffering, and even death. When they learn to enter the stories and meet God, they have a tool for living and discovering meaning in any place at any time.

Word and Action

Young children learn through their bodies as well as their minds. Movement, sight, sound, smell, sensing, feeling, taste, and touching are channels for their knowing. So the biblical stories need to be translated into figures and materials that children can see and move about, giving them a sensorimotor way of absorbing the story by repetition and also a means for responding to God.

In worship, word (liturgy) and movement (rubric) join mind and body in praising God. When scripture is read to us we hear the words, but the movement occurs in our minds, in our imagination. We picture the story and project ourselves into it. In this way, remembering happens. Children are helped to form images of scripture by receiving the story in visual and motor ways that allow kinesthetic, visual, and auditory thinking to happen.

This is one reason we translate the biblical stories and parables into materials children can see and move.

Moving the Figures

The same principle of using only the essentials and omitting the details applies to materials as well; we use as few as possible. One quickly learns how cumbersome and time-consuming it is to move what the imagination can move better. The figures are plain and without detail, particularly the faces, since children tend to focus on the face. They are moved with an economy of motion so as not to distract—usually in a smooth, gliding manner—instead of being jumped or bounced along.

The movement of the materials serves several functions. On the one hand it makes kinesthetic and visual thinking possible. The story is experienced through the hands, the fingers, and the body. It is also pictured mentally. Images are foundational for thinking and for the development of concepts and theological statements. One of the tasks of early childhood is the forming of images on which to build an identity and a worldview.

Sometimes the movement imitates the rubrics of worship, as when the story of the Last Supper is told. In this story the movement of Jesus taking, blessing, breaking, and giving the bread is like that of the celebrant in worship. So when children see similar gestures made in worship they will connect them with the stories. Also, storytellers and children alike discover that certain movements used in one story remind them of another story in which the same gestures are made. They reflect on the relationship of the two and thus take the beginning steps of doing theology.

Getting the materials from the shelves to the floor and putting them away is another function of movement. The movement of the leader to the shelf is the beginning of the story, while the return of the materials ends it. Since the materials serve as translations of the biblical stories or parables, one approaches them as a reader approaches the Bible to read it in worship. Without speaking, the storyteller carries the materials with both hands, as the Bible is carried in procession. This movement conveys a valuing of the materials and prepares the storyteller to enter the story. At the same time the silence fills a practical function in that the children must watch in order to learn where to get and return the materials. This enables them to move at will during the response time. Since putting the materials away is viewed as part of the story, the room remains orderly and children are calmer because they can find what they want.

Movement and the use of underlays help to focus and move the children into the world of the story. Stories are told on felt underlays or in the desert box, a 2-by-3-foot box, about three inches high, filled with sand. Using both hands, the leader smooths out the underlay or smooths and molds the sand in the desert box. This movement is essential for focusing the children's attention on the place that will become the context for the story. The rhythmic smoothing, joined with words of wondering what this could be, draws both storyteller and children into the story and transforms the sand or felt into the desert, the Jordan River, or the road to Jerusalem, and so on. We continue wondering as each necessary piece is laid out. By not discussing the children's responses but rather incorporating them into the story, we build a context for the parable while still wondering what it might really be and what will happen there.

All stories in the desert box begin, "This is the desert box. So many important things happen in the desert that we just have to have a small piece of it in our room. The desert is a strange and wild place. At night it is very cold, but in the day it is burning hot. There is almost no water at all. The desert is always changing. The wind comes. And as it blows it shapes and molds. So the desert is never the same."

During Advent, as we move our hands over the underlay we say, "This is the season of Advent, the time we get ready to celebrate the mystery of Christmas, the time we are *all* on the way to Bethlehem. But who will show us the way?"

During Lent most of the stories are told on the road to Jerusalem, so we say, "Once every year the people of God go up to Jerusalem, the holy city of God, to celebrate the feast of the Passover, to remember how God led them through the waters to freedom."

PREPARATION OF THE STORYTELLER

The preparation of the storyteller is of primary importance. The storyteller must personally own and sense the greatness, mystery, and awe of God in the story. It is best to have an experienced storyteller present the story to you first. Then read it from the Bible and meditate on it. When you feel the story has formed in you, turn to Part III in this book for the story and the directions for moving the materials. After reading it through once, reread the directions for moving the materials and try to visualize and feel the movement. Begin to practice the presentation by moving the materials without saying the words out loud. When you feel comfortable with the movements, begin saying the story aloud as you move the figures. Here mind and body, memory and movement, combine to communicate the story. Adults forget how much is learned through the body until we begin telling stories with movement. But young children are very aware of learning this way. Sometimes as the children listen and watch the story they move their hands, imitating the gestures of the storyteller.

As you practice, keep your eyes on the materials. You have entered the world of that story for the moment. Lifting your eyes will bring you out of that world. Since you also want the children to be drawn into the story, you will avoid eye contact while presenting the story, since eye contact brings both the children and you out of the story, causing you to relate to one another instead.

Usually you will not speak while moving the materials, lest verbal and visual thinking be confused. This allows the children to observe how to move the figures without having to concentrate on the words at the same time.

But silence serves another function. It gives space for the Holy Spirit to act in the imagination. Since the children are imagining the story, they themselves are moving in it. They are personally lost in time. They are Abram or Sarai walking through the desert. The silence and the slowness are part of the journey.

When you do speak, do so with an economy of words. Try to use only necessary words so the children will not be distracted or confused while trying to sort out the essentials from the details.

You also need to give attention to the sound and rhythm of your words, because sound and rhythm are important with auditory thinking. Speak slowly so the children can hear and picture the words. A rhythm appropriate to the story should be used. Often it will be the rhythm of breathing.

Response: Wonder and Art

In worship the time following the reading of scripture and the sermon is a time of response to the word. As we noted earlier, the response may take a variety of forms such as the singing of a hymn or the saying of a creed; baptism or confirmation; prayers of intercession; or an offering. The children's responses to the story vary also. Sometimes their response is sheer joy. Sometimes it is awe, wonder, or amazement. They enjoy wondering. So the period of time following the story allows first for a time for wondering together, then a personal response time for working with the story and art materials.

TIME FOR WONDERING

The time for wondering is a time of reflection, when the group engages in an open shared dialogue with the story, with one another, and with their experiences in the story. Wondering together is a community's way of remaining open to the Holy Spirit, a way of meditating so the story becomes a part of the group's life. As such, wondering shapes and deepens our knowledge of God and what God expects of us. It is a way the community of children come to know God and themselves. This knowing is based on their experience of God, not on being told about God. Their experience of God in the story informs their expression, and their expression, refined by the group, begins to name their world. This activity is the foundation on which theological thinking is built. The wondering together produces thinking Christians who can enter into dialogue, share their experiences of God, and together discover God's calling for them.

The storyteller makes reflection possible through the use of "wondering" questions. These questions keep the scripture open by dealing with the children's experience and understanding of the story. Thinking and dialogue would be stopped by questions that merely ask for details, such as "How many days did it rain?" or "How many times did Noah send out the dove?" Questions such as "I wonder how it felt to be in the ark in all that rain?" or "I wonder what it was like to be surrounded by so much water?" or "I wonder how they felt when they saw the rainbow?" permit reflection and enable anamnesis, not just the remembering of facts but the reliving of the experience. Wondering brings us to a knowledge of God, ourselves, and others in a deep and convincing way.

Asking Wondering Questions

Wondering questions come out of the depth of your experience in the story. You will try to ask questions that tie in with everyone's lived experiences. For example, we've all experienced being alone, so we can ask, after Jesus' temptation, "I wonder what it was like to be alone in the desert for such a long time?"

We have suggested questions after the stories to get you started. You don't have to use them all. Since the wondering time is a dialogue between you, the children, and God, you should listen with empathy to the children, respond in ways that keep the conversation open, and allow them to continue working with the ideas or the situation. You might say, "I wonder too. What do you think?" The children usually give their own solution. You might extend the conversation with questions such as: "Well, how could you do it?" or "I wonder what would happen?" Through active listening, help them come to knowing on their own.

Usually our wondering questions start with experiences at the beginning of the story and move through it, but they don't have to. Sometimes you might want to start at the end. Do whatever opens up ways to continue thinking about the story so the children don't think the Bible is closed. Knowing is not in whether they can recite back certain answers to detailed questions; rather, the knowing comes when they enter the stories in such a way that they enter into dialogue with God and the Christian community. The fruits of that knowing are lives being changed and renewed and the desire to share that experience with other people.

TIME WITH STORY AND ART MATERIALS

After the wondering comes time for a personal response, when the children may work with the story or art materials. Each child chooses what he or she wishes to do. Working with story materials gives children opportunity for repeating the story, telling it to one another, and, by moving the materials, to consider alternative actions. Sometimes they work with an experience in the story, as when a four-year-old boy crawled to the "city of Bethlehem." In the Advent-Christmas presentation a skyscape of the city of Bethlehem is placed at the end of a road. For the four Sundays of Advent the leader says, "We are *all* on the way to Bethlehem. But who will show us the way?" At last the procession—Isaiah, Mary and Joseph, the shepherds, and Magi—shows us the way; on Christmas they arrive at Bethlehem and encircle the newborn Christ child. During the response time the storyteller watched a little boy crawling toward Bethlehem, slowly but with determination. At last he arrived and, still on hands and knees, gazed at the infant. "I made it," he said. "I see Jesus."

Art Responses

The children are also encouraged to use art materials. Art responses enable the children to express understandings and work through critical issues they cannot or do not wish to express verbally. Sometimes they resolve personal problems through their art. The artwork may be a means of talking with God, a form of prayer. The children may experience healing and wholeness.

Sometimes children link or transfer learnings from other stories. For example, after the Abram and Sarai story a four-year-old girl produced a drawing with three altars on it and a large rainbow arching over the whole page. The leader, who thought the girl was just fascinated with rainbows, was surprised when the child said joyfully, "This is the rainbow over all the places Abram and Sarai went." This theological linkage would be difficult for her to explain in words. But it is clear from the drawing that she understood more than she could express through theological language.

Sometimes art and movement combine, as when after the presentation of the temptation of Jesus a typical *Star Wars* seven-year-old boy was working with a *red* ball of clay. He used some of the clay to make a small person. The rest he formed into a ball, which he proceeded to roll over the figure, flattening it. This seemingly violent activity continued. After a while he said, "I'm squooshing Satan so he can't bother Jesus anymore." After a moment, the leader asked, "I wonder who could really squoosh Satan?" The boy thought a bit and said, "Jesus." "Hmm," the leader responded. "I wonder how he would do it?" The leader was thinking of several ways, but not of the answer she was about to hear. The child was silent a moment and then said, "With love." Amazing. Seven-year-olds are not supposed to know that. Until then, it had never occurred to the storyteller. Was this the traditional "Jesus and love" answer of the Sunday school child? We don't know, but we do know that the adults who heard it were changed.

Sometimes the results are not immediately evident. One summer a colleague used this approach in an inner-city neighborhood program. During the parting blessing she placed a heart sticker on each child, saying, "God has put God's very own heart within you because God loves you. Go in God's love." While walking home, she heard a little girl shouting angrily at two others who were returning from the worship center. "I hate you!" she screamed. "You guys got me in trouble, and I had to stay in and couldn't go to church." In that neighborhood such matters are usually settled by a street fight. But not that day. The two girls who had just come from the worship center were dismayed and said very gently, "Oh, we're so sorry. Let's not talk about that now. Let's just be glad you can come out now." And they took her hands and walked down the street together.

As we have seen, the children's responses after the hearing of the story are varied. Some are expressions of praise and love. Some follow the invitation to come and see Jesus. Some make theological connections with other stories. Some enjoy the story so much they want to tell it again and again. The purpose, of course, is that they meet God, love and respond to God, and experience what it means to hear scripture as remembrance, a way of reliving and abiding in the presence of God.

PREPARING FOR THE RESPONSE TIME

The response time is not for free play. It is a personal time with the stories. The children need to have appropriate freedom to move and work in the room, but they must be shown how. Part II, "Getting Ready to Be with God," is designed to do this. We think of these four sessions primarily as the first part of the order of worship, where we prepare to approach God. In these sessions we learn how to get ready to listen and respond to God's stories. They are so important we have written them out in full, despite repetitions. They help the children practice how to move in the room; how to make a special place to work; how to get and return materials by themselves, and which materials they need to ask for help in moving, such as Mount Sinai; how to use the art materials; and how to ask for help.

Since this is a personal time for the children, the leaders must give them freedom to work on their own. Leaders do not entertain or interrupt the children's work by striking up a conversation, but they are available for help and for more wondering together upon request. However, if material is being misused the leader approaches the child and may retell the story if the child has not remembered it.

The children need the freedom to choose their own response instead of everyone doing the same artwork prepared by the leader. Sometimes when a child uses the art materials, there is no apparent response to the story. Some respond by reproducing the story, while some produce work that interprets it. Children will also use art to work through existential issues. Since these responses are personal, they should be told to the leader only if the child wishes and are received as a gift. The leader may ask if the child wants to tell about his or her work, but if not the leader does not probe. The children may keep both their finished and unfinished work in a file. When compiled over a period of time, their artwork functions like a spiritual journal and provides a way for the children to remember and build on their experiences in the stories.

How the Church Measures Time

There are many ways to tell time. Ordinarily we construct time around the movement of the sun. So we say a day is twenty-four hours and a year is 365 days. We divide the year into four seasons: spring, summer, fall, and winter. Sometimes time is told by the moon, as it was by nomadic people, who traveled in the cool of the night. Their days went from evening to morning. Sometimes time is mythical or metaphorical, like "once upon a time" or "for forty days and forty nights." Sometimes time is constructed by events: "In the beginning," or "In the year that King Uzziah died," or "It was the feast of Passover."

The church's year is Christological. It tells time by celebrating the events of Jesus' birth, life, death, resurrection, and ascension and the gift of the Holy Spirit. Using both solar and lunar time, the church year is basically composed of Sundays occurring in six seasons: Advent, Christmas, Epiphany, Lent, Easter, and Pentecost. These seasons are divided between two cycles, the Easter cycle and the Christmas cycle.

Easter is the oldest of the two church cycles. It is composed of Lent, Easter, and Pentecost. Rooted in the Jewish feasts of Passover and Pentecost, it is based on the lunar calendar, so the day of Easter falls on the Sunday after the first full moon on or after March 21. Since the full moon may occur any time between March 21 and April 18, Easter may occur any time between March 22 and April 25. Lent begins on Ash Wednesday forty days before Easter. Pentecost is on the Sunday fifty days after Easter.

The Christmas cycle is composed of the seasons of Advent, Christmas, and Epiphany. It is based on the solar calendar, and so Christmas always falls on December 25. Advent begins four Sundays before Christmas, and Epiphany is January 6, twelve days after Christmas.

Church time is "sacred" time with a story. And in sacred time, as we said earlier, memory, imagination, and meaning work together so we can celebrate the shared stories of God's activity in human history by remembering them as though they were happening to us. Memory enables us to remember and recall the story; imagination enables us to relive it, make it new again; and meaning interprets and applies it to our actions.

The *Common Lectionary* provides a system of readings for each Sunday, enabling Christians throughout the world to hear the same passages of scripture. The *Common Lectionary* provides a three-year cycle of three lessons for each Sunday as well as a three-year cycle for reading the Psalms. While there are exceptions, generally the first lesson is from the Old Testament, except during Easter, when it is from Acts. The psalm is a response to this lesson. The second lesson is usually from an epistle, and the third reading is from one of the Gospels.

To help young children learn to tell church time, we use a puzzle constructed in a circle, since church time marks beginnings that are endings and endings that are beginnings. We also place a large circle of the church year on the wall and move the pointer each Sunday. The puzzle helps young children learn the names of the days and the seasons and what is celebrated. They also learn the colors and the number of Sundays in each season as we change the liturgical cloths on the prayer table and under the Nativity figures. Basically, the liturgical colors are purple or blue for Advent, white for Christmas, white for Epiphany, green for the season after Epiphany, purple for Lent, white for Easter, red for the day of Pentecost, and green for the season after Pentecost.

With young children we tend to follow the church year thematically instead of following the lectionary. The Sundays where we do coincide are the Sunday after Epiphany, when we tell the baptism of Jesus; the first Sunday of Lent, when we repeat the temptation of Jesus in the wilderness; and Easter, when we tell Jesus' appearance to Mary. We tell the Emmaus story the second week of Easter instead of the third, but on the fourth Sunday we join in telling the Good Shepherd parable. The story of the Ascension is told on the seventh Sunday and the story of Pentecost on Pentecost Sunday.

STORIES FOR THE CHURCH YEAR

We begin in September with four sessions to orient the children to the worship center. In this time for getting ready to be with God, we do two things: we help the children learn to enter sacred time and place, and, since the children's response time depends on their ability to move with appropriate freedom in the room, we help them learn how to use the room "all by themselves." These sessions are absolutely essential to the well-being of the time together. In centers where they are hurried or skipped, everyone suffers from disruptions.

The first "Getting Ready" session is for both children and parents. It is held during the week, before the first regularly scheduled session. Because there is so much to practice, each session is limited to six children and their parents. You may have to run the session several times, depending on the size of your class. The next three sessions systematically build on the previous ones, so that by the fifth session you can move through the whole order of worship.

The Light

The first story is told in the fourth session. This is a liturgical story using the Christ candle and is based on Jesus' saying "I am the Light." We tell this first because children respond so meaningfully to it and because it links to baptism. Also, we use the Christ candle during the time we read the story from the Bible each week.

The Good Shepherd

Our next two sessions tell the parable of the Good Shepherd. (This parable is in three parts, but the third part, about the Good Shepherd and the wolf, is not told until after Easter.) The children construct their image of Jesus through the Good Shepherd. They relate to the security and safety provided by the Good Shepherd and the sheepfold. This story provides a link to the Lord's Supper.

Creation

From here we move to Old Testament narratives that form our identity as the people of God. We begin with Creation. We speak of it in terms of gift—God's gift of creation—and the special day of creation when we can remember all the gifts of creation.

Noah

In the story of Noah, adults tend to focus on the sin and destruction of the flood while children focus on the safety of the ark. The essential meaning for them is not in moving the animals two by two but will all be safe in the ark? The phrase "washed clean and new" relates to baptism. Altars are introduced as places to give thanks to God. Happiness and joy are linked to prayer as a response to the presence of God. The altar symbolizes a meeting place with the Holy and marks a high place where God spoke. The rainbow, of course, dominates the children's art.

Abram and Sarai

This story, while introducing God's call and covenant with Abram and Sarai, meets the need of children for knowing where God is. Like the Good Shepherd who walks in front of the sheep to show them the way, so Abram and Sarai discover that God journeys with them through the desert. God speaks to them in various places. The story helps them experience that God is not only in Haran but in every place and every time. Like Noah, they are so happy God is with them, they build an altar and pray their thanks. (This is the first story told in the desert box. Most of the Old Testament stories are told in the desert box.)

Exodus

The Exodus story deals with the existential issue of oppression and freedom. The children identify with being trapped and having to do whatever Pharaoh says. The phrase "through the waters to freedom" connects with baptism and is used again in the story of Jesus' baptism. Instead of building an altar, dancing as a form of prayer and praise is the response of the prophet Miriam and the people to their freedom.

The Ten Best Ways to Live

God showed the people of God the way through the water to freedom. Now that they were free they could go any way they wished, but what was the best way to go? Well, God loved them so much, God showed them the way to Mount Sinai, the Holy Mountain of God, and gave them the Ten Best Ways to Live, four best ways for loving God and six best ways for loving people. The tablets are heart-shaped and fit in a red heart box.

Ark and Tabernacle

The people loved the Ten Best Ways to Live so much they wanted a special place to keep them. So they made a beautiful golden box, called an ark. But then they needed a way to come near something so special, so they constructed a tabernacle around it. This became a holy place and time for being with God. It was a tent so it could travel with them, providing a place where a journeying people go to worship God. Just as a church building is important to our worship, so the tabernacle was the center of Israel's worship. Adults, especially, have difficulty with this story, since only the priest can go near the ark. This story is in sharp contrast to the stories of Advent, where *all* are on the way to Bethlehem to be near the Christ child. This story makes the incarnation, the ripping of the veil of the Holy of Holies at the crucifixion, and the principle of the priesthood of all believers more appreciated.

Entering the Promised Land

This story shows the fulfillment of God's promise of the land to Abraham. Here the Jordan River parts, as did the Red Sea, and the people of God go through the waters into the Promised Land. This links with the story of John baptizing Jesus in the Jordan, which we tell the first Sunday after Epiphany.

The Temple

Once the people of God had conquered the Promised Land and made Jerusalem their center, they built a house for God because they were no longer nomads, living in tents, but settled people living in houses. The Temple, constructed like the Tabernacle but larger, was the official place for worship. Many events in the life of Jesus took place at the Temple while he was there to celebrate the feasts. So the Temple is foundational to understanding the stories of scripture and its link to Christian places of worship.

Advent

Advent is the season of waiting for the coming of the Messiah. We await both the birth and the promised return of Christ. With young children we focus on meeting the Christ child through the birth narratives. We present this story liturgically, not chronologically. Like an advent wreath in a line, it uses candles and is told on a purple underlay, the color of Advent. We follow the structure of biblical birth narratives in which angels or messengers of God appear, saying, "Don't be afraid. Be happy. God is with you." And then the announcements: to Mary, "You will have God's special son," and to the shepherds, "God's special son is born."

Christmas

During the season of Christmas we celebrate the incarnation. The Advent scroll rolls out, ending in a white section where all the Nativity persons arrive at Bethlehem and encircle the Christ child. The movements are similar to Jesus' disciples moving around the table at the Last Supper. The getting ready and the movements contrast with the story of the Ark.

Epiphany

The season of Epiphany celebrates the manifestation of God through Jesus the Christ, a Light to the whole world. Since the church celebrates the baptism of Jesus on the first Sunday after Epiphany, we too begin with this story, followed by the Spirit's leading Jesus into the wilderness. Jesus returns from the wilderness and begins his ministry by proclaiming the kingdom of God, both through teaching and by mighty signs and wonders. We introduce the children to the proclamation of the kingdom of God through the parables of the Mustard Seed, the Leaven, the Great Pearl, the Sower, the Good Samaritan, and the Great Banquet.

While Jesus proclaimed the kingdom of God, he never defined the kingdom. Rather, he spoke of it in parables, which we find difficult to interpret. At one time people treated Jesus' parables as allegories. Later, biblical scholars decided parables were not allegories but illustrations, thought to have one main point. Current biblical scholarship holds that parables are extended metaphors. As metaphors, parables invite us into them in order to know and experience the reign of God. God is known indirectly by entering the parable and experiencing the reality within. In the parable we experience Jesus' experience of God. Knowledge of God comes by entering, not from standing outside and analyzing.

Parables are two-dimensional. There is the ordinary everyday dimension and a metaphorical dimension. The reign of God enters the ordinary everyday life of real people: shepherds, breadmakers, farmers, wealthy people, Samaritans. There are real places: Jerusalem, Jericho, homes, fields. In this ordinary world of human experience the kingdom of God enters and what seems impossible happens. We are invited to imagine a huge mustard shrub that provides safety, an enormous harvest from so much lost seed, selling everything for a pearl, a wealthy person inviting the poor to a feast. Such is life where God reigns. So of course parables are hard for us. The normal reaction is not to like them, to reject them, because they turn our world upside down. We are compelled to reject them or recompose our world.

The kingdom of God comes to us a gift of God. It cannot be earned. It is to be received as little children receive it. Since children are subjects in the kingdom, we can learn of God by listening to the children's stories of their experience of God in the parable as we wonder together.

The gold parable boxes look like precious gifts, because parables are very precious. The materials are flat because parables are two-dimensional and function differently from narratives. The children are invited into the parable as you begin laying out the underlay. They wonder verbally with you about each piece as you put it down. Don't discuss their suggestions. Rather, incorporate them into the story. You might ask, "I wonder what could be so white?" One might respond, "A snowball." You would say, "It might be a snowball." If suggestions come rapidly you don't need to repeat them. Just say, "It could be. I wonder," and move on.

Lent

Lent is a time of conversion, baptism, renewal, and discipleship. It is a time when we are *all* on our way to Jerusalem, and Jesus shows us the way, of preparing to share in his death and resurrection and, as his body, of continuing his ministry. It is a time when we review our Christian vocation to discern how we are specifically to be signs of God's kingdom in the world. The story of Jesus' temptation in the wilderness, which was told at Epiphany, is part of the lectionary reading for the first Sunday of Lent, so we retell it here. This is followed by stories of Jesus' healing Bartimaeus, the conversion of Zaccheus, and the triumphal entry. These three stories are told on the road to Jerusalem, which is placed on a purple felt underlay. (Purple is the color for Lent.) A skyscape of Jerusalem is at the end of the road, with an open gate for Jesus to ride through. On Passion/Palm Sunday we tell the story of Jesus' last supper with his disciples. The four actions of the Eucharist are the essential points. Jesus *took, blessed, broke,* and *gave* the bread to his disciples. These movements are the essential ones in the Lord's Supper and are necessary in the recognition of Jesus in the resurrection story of Emmaus. Jesus' death and resurrection are briefly told in relation to the supper. **Jesus' Last Passover** is told on a green underlay because it links with **The Good Shepherd** and **The Good Shepherd and the Lord's Supper.**

Easter

Easter is the joyful celebration of the death, resurrection, and ascension of Jesus. With the whole church we tell the story of Jesus' postresurrection appearance to Mary. The next week we tell of Jesus' appearance to the disciples at Emmaus. The structure of these stories is one of recognition and a response of proclamation. We tell the story in such a way that the children have the possibility, along with Mary, of recognizing Jesus as he calls her by name (a link with the Good Shepherd, who knows each of his sheep by name). And in the Emmaus story, Jesus is recognized when he does the same four actions of the Last Supper: take, bless, break, and give. Both stories contain words similar to the Easter greeting. "The Lord is risen. He is risen indeed." These stories are told on a white felt underlay, the color for Easter.

On the fourth Sunday of Easter, the lectionary uses the Good Shepherd story from John 10. So on the third Sunday we retell **The Good Shepherd and the Lost Sheep** and the fourth Sunday tell the third part of the parable, which includes the wolf. Now we are ready to link the Good Shepherd parable with the Lord's Supper. This story is told using three-dimensional figures on two green felt-covered circles. On one circle is a sheepfold with the sheep and the Good Shepherd. On the other is a table. The Good Shepherd calls the sheep from the sheepfold and walks in front of them to show them the way to the good green grass. Then, pausing where the two circles meet, the Good Shepherd moves over to the next circle and leads the sheep around his table, where he feeds them. The following week the story is repeated, and this time the sheep are exchanged for people, including children. One of the people of God, the celebrant, comes and says the words of the Good Shepherd. Thus the meaning of the sacrament of the Lord's Supper is experienced by the children. Just as they have entered the other stories and experienced God, so they enter this one and are fed by Christ, the Good Shepherd, at Christ's very own table. They are never more ready to partake of the Lord's Supper with the congregation.

Jesus' ascension is told liturgically, using the Christ candle and the historic affirmation, "Christ has died, Christ is risen, Christ will come again."

Pentecost

Pentecost and the season after Pentecost celebrate the gift of the Holy Spirit to the church, so that the body of Christ is empowered to proclaim and engage in the ministry and mission of Christ. On Pentecost Sunday the story of Pentecost is told. During the season after Pentecost we retell the story of the Light (found in Session 4) and the story of baptism.

THE ROOM

When the children enter the room, the "one story" of the Bible visually surrounds them. The materials for the stories, parables, and liturgical presentations just discussed are on the top shelves of low, open shelving. Materials that deepen the initial stories, such as books, puzzles, and other stories, are on the lower shelves.

The focal point of the room is the Nativity scene, the Holy Family with the donkey, shepherds, sheep, Magi, and camels. The shelf immediately underneath holds the liturgical cloths for each season that are used for changing the prayer table and the underlays for the Nativity scene. The Church Year puzzle is on the bottom shelf.

The shelves to the left and right as you face the Holy Family hold two other images of Christ. To the left is the Christ candle, the symbol of Christ the Light. Underneath are the materials used for the baptism presentations: a tray with candles, matches, and snuffer, a small baptismal bowl, a doll in a white gown, and cards with pictures of the baptism of a baby in sequence. To the right of the Holy Family is Christ the Good Shepherd and the sheep in the sheepfold. Underneath is the circle with the table of the Good Shepherd, a basket of wooden people, and a small box containing a beautiful miniature plate and cup.

To the left of the Christ candle are the liturgical materials for the Christmas cycle. For the Advent presentations there is a basket with four purple candles. (The white one for Christmas is always the Christ candle.) There is a tray with a long beautiful rolled-up purple cloth, made of velvet and divided into four sections on which the stories of Advent are told. This scroll helps connect the four Sundays of the season. It ends with a white section for Christmas. There is also a skyscape of Bethlehem. On the shelves underneath are puzzles and books. To the right of the Good Shepherd are the liturgical materials for the Easter cycle. Like the biblical story materials, these are three-dimensional because they are liturgical expressions of sacred stories.

On another section of shelves along another wall are the materials for the sacred stories. These are placed in biblical order on the top shelves. The lower shelves contain books, puzzles, and other materials that inform the stories. (Eventually they will contain other biblical stories that deepen the primary ones.) Between the Old Testament and New Testament shelves is an intertestament section on which a large Bible is placed. The desert box is stored underneath, on the floor. Next to this are the New Testament stories. The materials for the sacred stories are three-dimensional and are placed on trays or in baskets so the children can carry them easily. There is only one set for each story.

A third section of shelves placed along another wall holds the gold parable boxes. The leader moves laminated figures over felt underlays in telling the parables. It is like using a felt board on the floor.

On the shelves underneath the parable boxes are art materials: crayons, markers, chalk, paints, clay, scissors, cloth, paste sticks, several kinds of paper, towels, sponges, buckets, and various other supplies.

Rugs for each child are stacked or kept in a large box. These are used for defining each child's work space and for reading or resting.

In a quiet place in the room is a prayer corner with a small table covered with a cloth the color of the liturgical season. On the table is a Bible with bookmarks, each with a symbol of one of the stories so the children can locate the story in the Bible. The verses are underlined or highlighted so children can look at the words or ask someone to read them. Also on the table are a cross, candles, and flowers or other symbols appropriate to the season. For example, we have an Advent wreath during Advent.

Thus the room is organized visually and spatially so that the children have direct access to the biblical stories, parables, and liturgical expressions through the materials. In this way they indirectly experience the differences in religious language: the language of biblical narrative, which forms our identity as Christians; the language of parable, which turns our composed worlds upside down, bringing faith change; and the language of liturgy, which provides a balance between story and parable.

The church measures time by telling the stories of God in such a way that the one story is a story for all times and places. In church time, beginnings are endings and endings are beginnings. And so it is from generation to generation of those who love God.

Getting Started

In beginning this approach to children's worship in a congregation, it is helpful either to attend a "Children and Worship" workshop for training or to find a congregation that is using this approach and ask if you and another person from your congregation may visit their worship center. Make an appointment to meet with the worship leader and ask to have the Good Shepherd parable presented to you. You may want to take pictures of the room and the materials. Then decide how to gain the approval and support of your pastor and governing body or bodies.

An excellent way to introduce the appropriate governing board to this approach to young children and worship is briefly to share your experience and why you are excited about it. Invite everyone to sit on the floor, asking them to be themselves, not young children, but to allow themselves to find the child hidden in them. Then, just as you would do with the children, help them begin to transform the room into a place to be with God. Sing "O God, We Adore You" and "Be Still and Know That I Am God" to help quiet them inside. Then tell the Good Shepherd parable, including the wolf. They are usually so moved they are ready to listen, if not give wholehearted support. Spend some time reflecting and wondering on their experiences in the parable, and then ask them to return to their chairs to see slides of a worship center. Then submit a written proposal for the action you would like the board to take.

There are several things to decide. What age will you start with? How will you group the children? Should you cross the age span so three- to seven-year-olds are all together? (Some small churches are doing this with three- through twelve-year-olds!) How many groups will you need? If you are a large church you may want to begin with just three- and four-year-olds and phase in the program. An ideal size is about twelve children, but some of our centers have had as many as thirty-five.

Where will you do this? What kind of space is available? You need a quiet place free from loud and sudden noises.

How soon can you begin worship with children?

What will be your setting? Many are possible. Most churches do this on Sunday morning in relation to congregational worship or as an alternative to Sunday school. But there are a number of other settings. Two hours on a weekday is ideal because it gives the children a longer response time. A program held during the week could serve not only the children of your church but also the neighborhood children. It could be held after school, particularly for neighborhood children whose parents are at work. Or it might be worked into church-supported day care a couple of hours a week. (You would need a special room or section used only for this program.) Other possible settings would be Wednesday-evening family night or the Sunday-evening hour. We also know of people using this program with mentally impaired, blind, troubled, ill, and terminally ill children.

When you have permission to begin this program and have decided when, where, and for whom you will have it, you are ready to recruit a team. The size of the team varies, depending on the number of children you have. You will need at least one worship leader and one greeter for each group. If you have several groups you will need a director. You will also need a materials supply person who will purchase and make or find volunteers to make materials. Since the leader knows what kind of materials are needed, she or he usually wants to be involved in searching for them or making them.

WORSHIP LEADERS AND DIRECTORS

Recruit persons who love children and are easygoing. It might be better to find people who have a feel for worship and spiritual formation rather than trained teachers. The training for teaching and for leading worship differs, and it is sometimes hard for teachers to switch roles. Recruit both men and women. Tell them what is expected of them and the details of the commitment you are asking for. They will need training and support. Discuss whether they will go to a "Children and Worship" training center or be prepared by someone who has had the training.

Worship leaders and directors are responsible for interpreting children's worship to the parents and the congregation. The first year, the chairperson of the appropriate governing board will send a letter to the parents and the congregation to introduce you and this approach to children's worship. The letter to parents should include an invitation to an introductory meeting that the director or worship leader or an experienced person from another center will lead. It is important that the pastor and committee members be present to give their support. The presentation should be similar to the one given to the governing board.

Explain what is expected of parents and why. Help them understand and be at ease with the procedure of leaving their children at the door with the greeters and waiting outside the door when returning for them, rather than entering the room. Help them understand that the children are "at worship" and that the worship leader greets and says good-bye to each child personally.

Briefly explain the "Getting Ready" sessions. State the importance of the parents coming with their children to an orientation session. Then announce the dates and times for that first session. Have the schedule ready and ask them to sign for a time before they leave. You will need to follow through with confirmations and scheduling for those who did not sign or were not there. Be sure to mail a reminder or call a few days before the meeting.

Since interpretation to parents and congregation is ongoing, you might wish to have monthly or quarterly meetings where you present the stories, share what is happening with the children, and receive feedback from the parents.

Needless to say, a major responsibility of the worship leader is getting to know the children. Each child should be addressed by name.

GREETERS

Greeters are extremely important to the atmosphere and functioning of the worship center. They need to be trained too, so they understand how and why the worship center functions. Greeters are responsible for preparing the feast for each session and for asking two children to help. (They develop a system to give each child a turn.) They consult with the leader for suggestions for foods, to relate them to the story of the day. (For example, animal crackers or bread in the form of a dove might be eaten after the Noah story.)

The greeters meet the children and the parents at the door "in the name of the Lord." They should know each child by name. If not, they make a name tag before the parents leave.

When new children come, greeters learn their names and briefly tell the children and their parents what happens in the worship center. Then they walk with the children to the circle and introduce them to the worship leader.

At the door, greeters help children put things they've brought with them in the special place where such things don't get lost and can be picked up when they leave.

The greeters care for children who don't wish to be in the group. They may sit beside a child outside the group until the child feels ready to enter it. If a child is disruptive during the story, the greeter removes him or her quietly from the circle and stays with the child until the story is over and the child feels ready to return. Just as the worship leader is to be centered in God, so are the greeters as they care for the children. They function out of a centered quietness so each child feels the love and security of the caring person even if the child is out of control.

During the response time, greeters help children with paint shirts and carry material that is too heavy for them, but they do not entertain or interrupt the children's personal time with the story.

Greeters serve the feast. They give napkins and food to child helpers to pass out, but they distribute the juice themselves.

The greeters are at the door to meet parents when they return, and they tell each child when his or her parent is there. When all the children have gone, they help the leader straighten the room and make a list of supplies needed for next time.

THE MATERIALS PERSON

It is very important that the person or team making and securing materials understand how the worship center will be set up and how the materials function in the center. Although we are including here a list of items and the amount of fabric, trays, and baskets needed, materials supply persons should also read each story to visualize how the materials are used and study the materials lists. They will also be helped by visiting a "Children and Worship" center.

Materials supply persons should imagine the worship center as a place of worship but not as a sanctuary with pews in place. Rather, imagine it as a beautiful, peaceful, orderly place, with figures representing biblical stories on open shelves. The furnishings and materials are to be affordable but also beautiful. Since the materials represent biblical stories, parables, or objects used in congregational worship, they take on a special and sacred dimension. Of course the fabric is just felt, but it is special felt because it is a pasture or the road to Jerusalem. Of course it is just a piece of white satin under the Christ candle, but the meaning the Christ candle holds for us stirs us to prepare a beautiful place on which to set it.

It may take a great deal of imagination and searching to provide a beautiful room at low cost, but it can be done. Don't let the list of materials discourage you. In the first year, all our rooms were almost empty. We started with a few shelves or a low table, so at least we had a focal point, with the Christ candle and the Nativity set, and a place for the art materials. Those who didn't have shelves placed the materials on trays on the floor, and if they couldn't afford trays they used open boxes beautifully covered with paper the color of the church season, or just plain white open boxes. Gradually shelves, trays, baskets, and figures were added. For example, one worship center got free wood scraps from the shop at their high school, and someone in the congregation cut out the figures. People donated fabric. Since they could not afford a lot of trays at first, they placed the materials directly on the shelves and bought just a few trays. Then they showed the children how to get a tray, go get the figures, place them on the tray, carry them to their work space, remove the figures, and return the tray to its place so another child could use it.

When you are ready to purchase the material and shelves, have a plan for the whole room. Decide on the colors for the walls, carpet, shelves, baskets, and trays. They need to blend and look good together. The color of the walls and carpet are significant to the environment and the beauty of the center. It is good for walls to be painted an off-white or a light color, with a plain-colored, nontextured carpet, since the stories are told on the floor. Tan, brown, or beige carpeting looks best since it goes with the underlays for the stories, which are primarily dark blue, rust, yellow, purple, green, white, and red.

Wooden shelves and trays have the warmest feel to them and are attractive without calling attention to themselves. Use trays and baskets that are alike or similar, giving uniformity and a sense of order to the room. This focuses attention on the story materials rather than on the trays and baskets. The trays are important because they keep the materials for each story together and the children do not need to search for them. Also, trays allow the children to carry the materials to their workplace by themselves, usually in one trip.

The baskets are similar to each other: plain, with lids, round, oval, or square, depending on the size and number of the figures that go in them, and from 2½ to 7 inches in diameter and 2½ to 4 inches high. (We give our sizes; you will want to measure your figures and use your own judgment for substitutions to make them affordable.) You might want one kind of trays and baskets for all the Old Testament stories and another for the New Testament ones. We use our most beautiful trays and baskets for the liturgical materials, **Baptism**, and **The Lord's Supper**. The parables are stored in gold boxes.

The wooden figures are of plain pine. They are not painted, so the children can imagine how they look and feel.

When you begin, you do not want to have everything in the room. You only need the focal center materials: the Christ candle and materials for **The Light**,* the Nativity figures, and the art materials. When you are ready to tell the next story, add its materials to the center. The children will not know how to use the figures until they see and hear the story, so it's best not to have them in the room. The bareness does not bother the children. Rather, it gives them a chance to learn well how to use what's there and in the long run frees them to use the space appropriately and spares them from being overwhelmed.

The following lists will help your shopping. The amounts of fabric were determined with the least waste so you may want to cut all the pieces at once. You will need to think how to cut it so you can get all the pieces from it. For example, you will need 2 ⅓ yards of green felt, 72 inches wide. The following pieces need to come from it: Good Shepherd underlay, 36 by 36 inches; mustard tree, 30 by 30 inches; banquet underlay, 36 by 36 inches; Last Passover underlay, 24 by 48 inches; and Good Shepherd and Lord's Supper, 2 pieces, each 13 by 13 inches. It can be cut like this:

---

*Be sure to check your local fire code before using candles in the building.

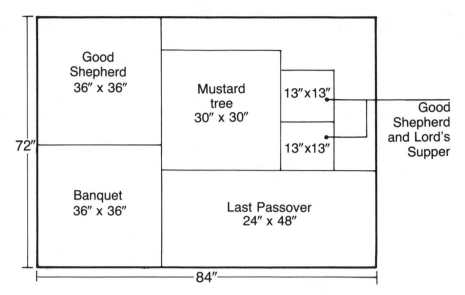

MATERIALS FOR THE WORSHIP CENTER

LITURGICAL MATERIALS

Candles
White
Christ candle: 1	$3'' \times 9''$ or larger
Light: 1 for each child	$\frac{3}{4}''-1'' \times 8''$ or $9''$

Purple (or blue): 4
Advent	$2\frac{1}{2}'' \times 8''$ or larger

Supplies
Candle snuffers: 3

Candle holders (to fit candle sizes chosen)
For Christ candle: 1
For each child, as many as needed

Glass match containers (with covers)
Advent: 1
Light and Baptism: 1

Safety matches: 2 packages

RUGS

Use samples or inexpensive beige towels	1 for each child 1 for two children	If all work is done on floor If tables are used

FIGURES FOR SACRED STORIES

Lauri puzzle "Kids" #2120 (19 figures) or use patterns in Part IV	2	Abram and Sarai
	7, plus one for each child	Exodus
	1	Ark and Tent for God
	11, plus one for each child	Promised Land
	6	Exile

BUILDINGS AND BACKGROUNDS

Desert box	24"×36"×4" deep	Wood or plastic, filled with clean sand
Noah's ark		Noah
Haran		Abram and Sarai
Tabernacle		Ark and Tent for God
Solomon's Temple		Temple
City of Jericho		Promised Land
Herod's temple		Jesus in the Temple; Jesus in the Wilderness
City of Bethlehem (skyscape)		Advent
City of Jerusalem with gateway		Lent
Backdrop of Jericho		Lent
Clay tomb		Appearance to Mary
Upper room backdrop		Jesus' Last Passover
Emmaus house backdrop		Road to Emmaus

ROCKS AND STONES

For mountains	2	Ten Best Ways to Live; Jesus in the Wilderness

For altars	24 to 29	Noah; Abram and Sarai; Promised Land (12)
Other	3	Jesus in the Wilderness

PAPER, CARDBOARD, ADHESIVES

Mat board (white), 32"×40": 2 sheets

Church Year Puzzle	24"×30"
Advent	24"×24"
	8"×40"

Poster board, 32"×40" (include at least one extra sheet for children to use with Creation)

White: 4 sheets

Creation	6"×8" (cut 2)
Ten Best Ways to Live	8"×11" (cut 2)
Christmas	7"×8½"
Backing for parables	8½"×11" (cut 23)

Purple: 2 sheets

Advent	7"×8½" (cut 4)
Purple Advent	24"×24"

Dark blue: 2 sheets   6"×8" (cut 2)

Royal blue: 2 sheets   6"×8" (cut 2)

Light blue: 2 sheets   6"×8" (cut 2)   } Creation cards

Green: 2 sheets   6"×8" (cut 2)

8"×11" (cut 2) Law

Construction paper, 9"×12" (order extra for children)

Yellow: 9 sheets   6"×8" (cut 16) Creation
3"×4½" Advent

White: 2 sheets   6"×8" (cut 2) Creation
3"×6" Advent

Green: 2 sheets   6"×8" (cut 2) Creation
8½"×11" Advent

Royal blue: 1 sheet   6"×8" (cut 2)

Tan: 1 sheet   6"×8" (cut 2)   } Creation

Purple: 1 sheet   8½"×11"

Gold: 1 sheet   4"×4½"   } Advent

Laminating paper, 12″ wide: approx. 15 yards

Adhesives
    1 can of fabric glue
    1 can of spray glue
    Paste sticks (1 for every two children)

FABRICS

Felt (72″ wide)

Green: 2⅓ yards

Good Shepherd	36″×36″
Mustard Seed	30″×30″
Great Banquet	36″×36″
Last Passover	24″×48″
Good Shepherd and Lord's Supper	13″×'3″ (cut 2)

Light blue: ⅓ yard

Good Shepherd	8″×11″

Dark blue: 1¼ yards

Good Shepherd	5½″×11″
Creation	15″×72″
Noah	24″×36″
Exodus	6″×24″ (cut 2)
Promised Land	6″×24″ (cut 2)
Jesus Is Baptized	6″×44″
	6″×22″
Good Samaritan	8″×11″

Tan: ⅚ yard

Good Shepherd	1″×14″ (cut 12)
Leaven	30″×36″

Cream or beige: 2⅔ yards

Jesus in Temple	6″×45″
On the Road to Jerusalem	8″×96″
Appearance to Mary	4″×30″
Road to Emmaus	6″×45″

White: 2¼ yards

Church Puzzle	24″×30″
Great Pearl	40″×40″
Appearance to Mary	34″×36″
Road to Emmaus	24″×45″

Yellow: 1 yard

Mustard Seed	36″×36″

Rust: 1/3 yard
Sower   12"×57"

Purple: 2 1/2 yards
Lent stories   18"×96"
                                               24"×24"

Medium brown: 2/3 yard
Jesus in Temple   24"×45"

Red: 2/3 yard
Pentecost   24"×36"

Satin (45" wide)

White: 1 yard plus table cover
Light   24"×36"
Lenten bag   9"×12"
Nativity   18"×24"
Christ candle   10"×12"
Prayer table   size to cover top

Purple: 1 yard plus table cover
Advent (can use blue)   18"×33"
Nativity   18"×24"
Prayer table   size to cover top

Green: 1/2 yard plus table cover
Nativity   18"×24"
Prayer table   size to cover top

Red: 1/2 yard plus table cover
Nativity   18"×24"
Prayer table   size to cover top

Burlap (36" wide)

Dark brown: 1 yard
Good Samaritan   36"×36"

Beige: 1 1/3 yards
Good Samaritan   6"×48"

Purple: 1/4 yard
Lenten Puzzle   9"×12"

Velvet (45" wide)

Purple: 1/2 yard
Advent   12"×45"
Jesus Is King   5"×8" (cut 5)

White: 1/3 yard
Advent   12"×12"

Cotton or lining fabric (36" wide)

Purple: 1 1/3 yards
Advent	12"×45"
Jesus Is King	5"×8" (cut 5)

White: 1/3 yard
Advent   12"×12"

Various pieces
Jesus Is King   3"×4" (1 for each child)

White brocade for Advent (1" wide): 1 2/3 yards

Gold drawstring for Lenten Puzzle bag: 1 1/4 yards

CONTAINERS

File folders with holder		One for each child's work
Rug box or basket		
Trays		
Bamboo, 12"×18"	17	One for each Old Testament and New Testament story
Wood, 12"×16"	8	Advent, Light, Baptism, Appearance to Mary, Road to Emmaus, Good Shepherd and Lord's Supper, Pentecost, and liturgical cloths
Clear stacking, 9"×12"	3	Creation cards and larger figures
Serving	2 to 4	For feast
Individual		One for each child's art supplies
Baskets		
Round 2"–2 1/2"	7	Creation
	1	Great Pearl (satin-covered)
2 1/2"–3"	3	Last Passover, Road to Emmaus, Lord's Supper
3"	3	Ark, Mustard Seed, Sower
4"	10	Abram and Sarai, Noah (3), Exile, Jesus in Wilderness, Mustard Seed (2), Leaven (2)

5"	17	Abram and Sarai, Exodus, Ten Best Ways, Ark, Promised Land (2), Jesus in Temple (2), Jesus Is Baptized (2), Jesus and Children, Bartimaeus (2), Zacchaeus, Appearance to Mary (2), Road to Emmaus, Lord's Supper
6"	7	Ark, Promised Land, Sower, Jesus and Children, Jesus the King (2), Pentecost
7"	5	Noah, Zacchaeus, Last Passover, Lord's Supper, Pentecost
Oval 2" × 4"	1	Noah
9" × 13"	2	Advent/Christmas

Boxes

Business envelope, 10" × 13"	7	One for each parable (gold-foil-covered)
Red hearts 2" × 2"	1	Ten Best Ways (small tablets)
7" × 8"	1	Ten Best Ways (large tablets)

PART II

GETTING READY
TO BE WITH GOD

This section contains four "Getting Ready" sessions. The sessions build on each other, so they are written in full to give you an idea of how to do this. For some of you the repetition may seem unnecessary, but it is important for young children. Move slowly and carefully through these sessions, because they set the atmosphere and foundation for the year. You may have to repeat part of them periodically.

The Worship Center Order, on gray paper, gives the format for all the rest of the sessions. You will move between it and the stories each week. Start by using its first paragraph, on preparation for worship, for the four "Getting Ready" sessions that follow here.

1

Orientation
to the Worship Center

A Very Special Place to Be with God

Greet each of the six children and their parents as they sit down on the circle. When all are present, help them transform the center into a special place by saying:

The Worship Center is a very special place. It is a special place to be with God. In this place we have all the time we need. So we don't need to hurry. We can walk more slowly. And we talk more softly, because someone might be talking with God, and we don't want to disturb them. This is a special place to be with God, to talk with God, to listen to God, and to hear the stories of God. So we need a way to get ready to be in such a special place to be with God. You can get ready all by yourself. You don't need me to tell you to get ready. But I can show you how to get ready to be with God.

We Walk More Slowly

When we come into this room we have all the time we need. So we can walk more slowly. Watch, I will show you how to walk.

Without talking, demonstrate how to walk by slowly placing one foot in front of the other. Walk to the door. Stop, turn around, and return. Sit down on the circle and cross your legs.

Now I wonder if you can show me how to walk in this room?

Give each child a turn to walk to the door and back.

We Sit on the Circle

Another way to get ready to hear the stories of God is to sit on the tape on the circle. We have a special way to sit. We cross our legs. Watch.

Demonstrate slowly, again without talking, how to sit with your legs crossed, with your hands on your knees or in your lap.

Now I wonder if you can show me the special way to sit in this room?

Give the children each a turn to sit with their legs crossed and their hands on their knees or in their laps.

We Speak More Softly

Another way to get ready is to speak with a soft voice. We speak softly because we do not want to disturb someone who may be talking to God. I can say my name softly. Listen: My name is _____. Now I wonder if you can show me how you say your name softly?

Give each child a turn to say his or her name softly.

We Talk to God

There are different ways to talk to God. One way is singing. When we're with God, we're so happy we just have to tell God. So we can sing our thanks. Here's a song we can sing.

Sing one verse of "O God, We Adore You" alone. Then ask the children to sing with you.

We Work with the Stories of God

When you walked around the room today, you saw some things on the shelves. The next time you come, you will be able to use some of them. When you use these materials you need a special place in the room. You can make a special place with a rug. I will show you how to get a rug. Watch.

Without talking, get up and walk slowly to the rug box. Pick up a rug with both hands. Place it over your shoulder and hug it. Walk back slowly, hugging your rug. Then place it on the floor and move to the end of it. Say:

I will show you how to unroll your rug. Watch.

Unroll the rug without talking. Smooth it out and sit on it. Say:

When you are on this rug no one will bother you. I will show you how to walk around a rug someone else is using. Watch.

Slowly walk around the rug, putting one foot in front of the other, without talking. Then say:

When you are finished working, you can put the rug away all by yourself. I will show you how. Watch.

Move to one end of the rug and silently roll it up. Pick it up with both hands and put it over your shoulder, hugging it. Walk slowly to the rug box and carefully, using both hands, put the rug in the box. Return silently and slowly (still showing how to walk) to the circle.

Now, I wonder if you can show me how to get a rug to make a special place to work?

Give each child a turn to get a rug, roll it out, sit on it, walk around it, roll it up, and put it away.

We Have a Feast

After we put our work away it is time to get ready for a feast. First we get ready by crossing our legs, so we will always know where they are when the food comes. Let's cross our legs now.

Now we need a table for our feast. I will show you how to make a table. Watch.

Take a large white paper napkin and place it in front of you on the floor. Silently and slowly, unfold it. Smooth it out with both hands. Then a greeter distributes napkins to the others, including the parents.

Now you can show me how to make a table for the feast.

When everyone has made a table, say:

Now it is time to thank God for our feast. Today I will say the prayer. Another day you may say the prayer.

Say a prayer of thanksgiving.

Today our feast is apples, cheese, crackers, and juice. You may have one of each. Put them on your table like this and wait until everyone is served. Watch.

The greeter serves you first so you can demonstrate what to do. When all are served, say:

Let us enjoy the feast together.

Have a joyful time of conversation, and when all are finished, say:

Now I will show you how to put away your table. Watch.

Take the paper juice cup off your napkin. Gather the four corners of the napkin together. Then put the napkin into the cup. Say:

Now [name of greeter] will come with the wastebasket for your cup.

Place your cup in the wastebasket.

We Go in God's Name

The next time you come, someone will bring you to this special place to be with God. When it is time to go, someone will come for you. We have a special way to say good-bye. [Name of greeter] will come to you and say, " [Name] is here for you." I want to say good-bye to each of you and give you a blessing. So first come to me so we can say good-bye and I can bless you.

Let's practice doing this now. First your parents will go stand by the door, so we can pretend they are just coming to get you. Then, as [name of greeter] tells you, you come here to me and then walk to your parents by the door.

Following the greeter's words, each child goes to the leader, is touched, and is given a positive, personal word and then a benediction. This is done quietly so no one but the child hears. End by saying to each child:

God go with you. Go in peace.

2

Talking to God

A Very Special Place to Be with God

Greet each child as he or she sits down on the circle. When all are present, help them transform the center into a special place by saying:

The Worship Center is a very special place. It is a special place to be with God. In this place we have all the time we need. So we don't need to hurry. We can walk more slowly. And we talk more softly, because someone might be talking with God, and we don't want to disturb them. This is a special place to be with God, to talk with God, to listen to God, and to hear the stories of God. So we need a way to get ready to be in such a special place to be with God. You can get ready all by yourself. You don't need me to tell you to get ready. But I can show you how to get ready to be with God.

We Walk More Slowly

When we come into this room we have all the time we need. So we can walk more slowly. Watch, I will show you how to walk.

Without talking, demonstrate how to walk by slowly placing one foot in front of the other. Walk to the door. Stop, turn around, and return. Sit down on the circle and cross your legs.

Now I wonder if you can show me how to walk in this room?

Ask a child to walk to the door and back. If there are new children, give each a turn.

We Sit on the Circle

Another way to get ready to hear the stories of God is to sit on the tape on the circle. We have a special way to sit. We cross our legs. Watch.

Demonstrate slowly, again without talking, how to sit with your legs crossed, with your hands on your knees or in your lap.

Now I wonder if you can show me the special way to sit in this room?

Give all new children a turn to sit with their legs crossed and their hands on their knees or in their laps.

We Speak More Softly

Another way to get ready is to speak with a soft voice. We speak softly because we do not want to disturb someone who may be talking to God. I can say my name softly. Listen: My name is _____. Now I wonder if you can show me how you say your name softly?

Give each child a turn to say his or her name softly.

We Greet One Another

Another way we get ready is to greet one another. I will say, "The Lord be with you" and you will say, **"And also with you."** Let's greet each other.

L: The Lord be with you.
C: And also with you.

We will greet one another this special way each time we come.

We Talk to God

There are different ways to talk to God. One way is singing. When we're with God, we're so happy we just have to tell God. So we can sing our thanks. Here's a song we can sing.

Sing the first verse of "O God, We Adore You" twice with the children.

Another way we talk to God is through artwork. We can draw our thanks to God. This is how you can get ready to talk to God through your artwork. First you need a special place.

If you are using tables instead of the floor for artwork, omit this step.

You can make a special place with a rug. I will show you how to get a rug. Watch.

Without speaking, walk slowly to the rug box. Pick up a rug with both hands. Place it over your shoulder and hug it. Walk back slowly, hugging your rug. Then place it on the floor and move to the end of it. Say:

I will show you how to unroll your rug. Watch.

Unroll the rug without talking. Smooth it out and sit on it. Say:

When you are on this rug no one will bother you. I will show you how to walk around a rug someone else is using. Watch.

Slowly walk around the rug, putting one foot in front of the other, without talking. Then say:

Now I will show you how to get your art materials. Watch.

Walk slowly to the art material shelves and silently pick up an empty tray. Set it down. Pick up a piece of paper and put it on the tray. Then pick up some crayons. Pick up the tray with both hands and carry it carefully to your rug. Do not talk while you are doing this. If you are using tables, demonstrate how to place the tray on a table, pull out the chair, sit down, and pull in your chair. Then demonstrate ways to use crayons.

When you are finished with your work, you may put it in your special folder. It will be there the next time you want it. We don't lose children's work here.

Silently walk to the shelf where the folders are and put your work in a folder. Return to your working place. If you are using tables, demonstrate how to push back your chair, get out of your chair, push your chair under the table, pick up your paper, and walk to the folders.

Now I will show you how to put your art materials away. Watch.

Check to see the crayons are on the tray. Then pick up the tray with both hands and carry it carefully to the art material shelf. Put the crayons in their place. Put the tray in its place. Do this without talking. Return to the circle.

When you are finished working, you can put the rug away all by yourself. I will show you how. Watch.

Move to one end of the rug and silently roll it up. Pick it up with both hands and put it over your shoulder, hugging it. Walk slowly to the rug box and carefully, using both hands, put the rug in the box. Return silently and slowly (still showing how to walk) to the circle.

Before you go to your work I want to show you two more things. This is what to do if you want to talk to me or need help. Look to see where I am and then walk to me and touch my shoulder.

Ask two children to demonstrate this.

If I am helping someone else, you may stand or sit by us and wait. Then I will listen to you. When I want to talk to you, I will dim the lights [turn the lights off and on again]. You are to stop working and look at my eyes. Let's try that now.

Walk to the light switch and signal with the lights. Look at all the children's eyes. Return to the circle.

Now, I wonder what work you would like to do today? You could make a special picture to help make this room beautiful. It could be something you want to thank God for. It could be something you want to show to God or tell God.

Ask the first child to get a rug. When the first child has a rug ask the next to go, and so on around the circle. Don't worry if this takes a long time. If they don't learn to do it now, you will have confusion the rest of the year.

Have a special chair to sit in while the children are working. Don't interrupt them. Let them come to you if they need help.

When it is time to get ready for the feast, use the light switch (or another signal). When you have their attention, say:

> Now it is time to get ready for the feast. You don't need to hurry. If you're not finished, that's all right. You can put your work in your special folder and finish it the next time you're here. We don't lose children's work in this place.

Return to your place in the circle and wait for the children to gather. The greeter(s) help if needed.

We Have a Feast

> It is time to get ready for a feast. First we get ready by crossing our legs, so we will always know where they are when the food comes. Let's cross our legs now. . . . We need a table for our feast. I will show you how to make a table. Watch.

Take a large white paper napkin and place it in front of you on the floor. Silently and slowly, unfold it. Smooth it out with both hands. Then a greeter distributes napkins to the others.

> Now you can show me how to make a table for the feast.

When everyone has made a table, say:

> Now it is time to thank God for our feast. Each of you may say thank you to God out loud. Or if you don't want to talk out loud to God, that's all right too. God listens even if we don't speak out loud. To help us get ready we get very still, and then we say:
>
> **L:** Let us give thanks to the Lord our God.
> **C: It is right to give thanks and praise.**
> **L:** Let us pray.

Be at home in the silence. After the children have finished, close with your prayer of thanksgiving.

> Today our feast is cheese, crackers, grapes, and juice. You may have one of each. Put them on your table like this and wait until everyone is served. Watch.

The greeters serve you first so you can demonstrate what to do. When all are served, say:

Let us enjoy the feast together.

Have a joyful time of conversation, and when all are finished, say:

Now I will show you how to put away your table. Watch.

Take the paper cup off your napkin. Gather the four corners of the napkin together. Then put the napkin into the cup. Say:

Now [name of greeter] will come with the wastebasket for your cup.

Place your cup in the wastebasket.

We Go in God's Name

When it is time to go home, we have a special way to say good-bye. [Name of greeter] will come to you and say, " [Name] is here for you." I want to say good-bye to each of you and give you a blessing. So first come to me so we can say good-bye and I can bless you.

Here is a song we can sing to each other while we wait:

Sing "Go Now in Peace" and then ask the children to sing with you. Each child comes to you and is touched and given a positive, personal word and then a benediction. This is done quietly so no one but the child hears. End by saying to each child:

God go with you. Go in peace.

3

Listening to God

A Very Special Place to Be with God

Greet each child as he or she sits down on the circle. When all are present, help them transform the center into a special place by saying:

The Worship Center is a very special place. It is a special place to be with God. In this place we have all the time we need. So we don't need to hurry. We can walk more slowly. And we talk more softly, because someone might be talking with God, and we don't want to disturb them. This is a special place to be with God, to talk with God, to listen to God, and to hear the stories of God. So we need a way to get ready to be in such a special place to be with God. You can get ready all by yourself. You don't need me to tell you to get ready. But I can show you how to get ready to be with God.

We Walk More Slowly

When we come into this room we have all the time we need. So we can walk more slowly.

Ask a child to walk to the door and back. If there are new children, give each a turn.

We Sit on the Circle

Another way to get ready to hear the stories of God is to sit on the tape on the circle. We have a special way to sit. We cross our legs.

Ask a child to show how we sit. Give all new children a turn to sit with their legs crossed and their hands on their knees or in their laps.

We Speak More Softly

Another way to get ready is to speak with a soft voice. We speak softly because we do not want to disturb someone who may be talking to God. I can say my name softly. Listen: My name is _____.

Give all new children a turn to say their names softly.

We Greet One Another

Another way we get ready is to greet one another. I will say, "The Lord be with you" and you will say, **"And also with you."** Let's greet each other.

Say the greeting two or three times. Use signing if you wish.

L: The Lord be with you.
C: And also with you.

We will greet one another this special way each time we come.

We Talk to God

There are different ways to talk to God. One way is singing. We can sing our thanks to God. Let's sing this song.

Sing two verses of "O God, We Adore You" alone. Then have the children sing with you.

Another way we talk to God is through artwork. We can draw our thanks to God. This is how we get ready to talk to God through our artwork.

First you need a special place. [Child's name], will you show how to get a rug to make a special place in front of me?

(If you are using tables instead of the floor for artwork, omit this step.) When the rug is smoothed out in front of you, say:

Watch closely where I go so you will know where the paper and markers and chalk are.

Walk slowly to the art material shelves and silently pick up an empty tray. Set it down and pick up a piece of paper and put it on the tray. Then pick up some markers and some chalk. Pick up the tray with both hands and carry it carefully to your rug (or table). Do not talk while you are doing this. Then demonstrate ways to use markers and chalk.

When you are finished with your work, you may put it in your special folder. It will be there the next time you want it. We don't lose children's work here.

Silently walk to the shelf where the folders are and put your work in a folder. Return to your place. (If you are using a table, follow the instructions in Session 2.)

Now I will show you how to put your art materials away. Watch.

Check to see the markers and chalk are on the tray. Then pick up the tray with both hands and carry it carefully to the art materials shelf. Put the markers and chalk in their places. Put the tray in its place. Do this without talking. Return to the circle. Go to one end of your rug and say:

Watch.

Then silently roll the rug up. Pick it up with both hands and put it over your shoulder, hugging it. Walk slowly to the rug box and carefully, using both hands, put the rug in the box. Return silently and slowly (still showing how to walk) to the circle.

Before you go to your work, let's remember what to do if you want to talk to me or need help. [Child's name], will you show us what to do if you need help or want to talk to me?

When the child is finished, say:

This is what I do if I want to talk to you.

Walk to the light switch, signal with the lights, and look at all the children's eyes. Then return to the circle.

Now I wonder what work you would like to do today? You could make a special picture to help make this room beautiful. It could be something you want to thank God for. It could be something you want to show to God or tell God. You may use crayons, markers, or chalk. [Child's name], what would you like to use?

While the first child is getting a rug (or materials), ask the next child what he or she would like to do. Continue one at a time around the circle. Don't worry if this takes a long time. If they don't learn to do this now, you will have confusion the rest of the year. When it is time to get ready for the feast, use the light switch (or another signal). When you have their attention, say:

Now it is time to put your work away. You don't need to hurry. If you're not finished that's all right. You can put your work in your special folder and finish it the next time you're here. We don't lose children's work in this place.

Return to your place in the circle and wait for the children to gather. The greeters will help if needed.

We Listen to God

One of the ways we come close to God is by becoming very quiet and listening. Quietness comes from inside you, not from someone telling you to be quiet. You can get quiet all by yourself. Some people like to sing to help them get quiet. We can sing "Be Still and Know That I Am God."

Sing and sign the song.

Some people like to make their bodies very still to help them get quiet. This is how. First, see if you can make your feet very still. . . . See if you can make your legs get very still. . . . Feel your body getting very still. . . . Now your arms are getting very still. . . . Now your head is very still. . . . Now your breathing is very still. . . . You can't hear it at all. . . . Breathe in . . . and out . . . in . . . and out.

Some people like to close their eyes to help them get quiet. Close your eyes and feel yourself floating on a cloud. Maybe you feel light . . . like a feather. Maybe you feel filled with air . . . like a balloon. Now Jesus is coming to you. . . . He takes your hand. . . . And you climb up into his lap. . . . Jesus hugs you. . . . He talks to you . . . then you talk to him. . . . Jesus talks . . . and you answer. . . . Jesus is talking again. . . . *(Silence)* . . . Now Jesus says, "It is time for the feast." Jesus hugs and kisses you good-bye and says, "Go in peace." . . . Now you can still enjoy the silence, and whenever you are ready you may open your eyes.

We Have a Feast

It is time to get ready for a feast. Let's get our legs ready. . . . Now let's get our tables ready.

When everyone has made a table, say:

Now it is time to thank God for our feast. Each of you may say thank you to God out loud. Or if you don't want to talk out loud to God, that's all right. God listens even if we don't speak out loud. To help us get ready, we get very still and then we say:

L: Let us give thanks to the Lord our God.
C: It is right to give thanks and praise.
L: Let us pray.

Be at home in the silence. After the children have finished, close with your prayer of thanksgiving.

Today our feast is [describe]. You may have one of each. Put them on your table like this and wait until everyone is served. Watch.

The greeter serves you first so you can demonstrate what to do. When all are served, say:

Let us enjoy the feast together.

Have a joyful time of conversation. When all are finished, say:

Now I will show you how to put away your table. Watch.

Silently take the paper cup off your napkin. Gather the four corners of the napkin together. Then put the napkin into the cup. Say:

Now [name of greeter] will come with the wastebasket for your cup.

Place your cup in the wastebasket.

We Go in God's Name

When it is time to go home, we have a special way to say good-bye. [Name of greeter] will come to you and say, " [Name] is here for you." I want to say good-bye to each of you and give you a blessing. So first come to me so we can say good-bye and I can bless you.

We can sing "Go Now in Peace" while we are waiting.

Each child comes to you and is touched and given a positive, personal word and then a benediction. This is done quietly, so no one but the child hears. End by saying to each child:

God go with you. Go in peace.

4

Listening to One of God's Stories:
The Light

A Very Special Place to Be with God

Greet each child as he or she sits down on the circle. When all are present, help them transform the center into a special place by saying:

The Worship Center is a very special place. It is a special place to be with God. In this place we have all the time we need. So we don't need to hurry. We can walk more slowly. And we talk more softly, because someone might be talking with God, and we don't want to disturb them. This is a special place to be with God, to talk with God, to listen to God, and to hear the stories of God. So we need a way to get ready to be in such a special place to be with God. You can get ready all by yourself. You don't need me to tell you to get ready. But I can show you how to get ready to be with God.

We Walk More Slowly

When we come into this room, we have all the time we need. So we can walk more slowly.

Ask a child to walk to the door and back. If there are new children, give each a turn.

We Sit on the Circle

Another way to get ready to hear the stories of God is to sit on the tape on the circle. We have a special way to sit. We cross our legs.

Ask a child to show how we sit. Give all new children a turn to sit with their legs crossed and their hands on their knees or in their laps.

We Speak More Softly

Another way to get ready is to speak with a soft voice. We speak softly because we do not want to disturb someone who may be talking to God. I can say my name softly. Listen: My name is _____.

Give all new children a turn to say their names softly.

We Greet One Another

Another way we get ready is to greet one another. I will say, "The Lord be with you" and you will say, **"And also with you."** Let's greet each other.

Say and sign the greeting two or three times.

> **L:** The Lord be with you.
> **C: And also with you.**

We will greet one another this special way each time we come.

We Talk to God

There are different ways to talk to God. One way is singing. We can sing our thanks to God. Let's sing this song.

Sing two verses of "O God, We Adore You" with the children.

We Listen to God

We listen to God by becoming very quiet. Quietness comes from inside you, not from someone telling you to be quiet. You can get quiet all by yourself. Some people like to sing to help them get quiet. We can sing "Be Still and Know That I Am God."

Sing the song once alone. Then ask the children to sing with you.

Some people like to make their bodies very quiet. This is how. Close your eyes and listen to the quietness. . . . Now see if you can make your feet get very still. . . . See if you can make your legs get very still. . . . Feel your body getting very still. . . . Now your arms are getting very still. . . . Now your head is very still. . . . Now your breathing is very still. . . . You can't hear it at all. . . . Breathe in . . . and out . . . in . . . and out. Now we are ready to listen to God, to hear one of God's stories. This is a story about the Light. Watch.

We Listen to One of God's Stories: The Light (John 8:12)

Turn to the liturgical shelf behind you and get the white satin underlay. Unfold it and smooth it out in front of you. Get the Christ candle and place it in the center of the cloth. Then get the tray with the smaller white candles, candle holders, matches, and candle snuffer. Hide the matches in your hand. Sit quietly while you feel the story forming in you. Then say:

Once there was someone who said such amazing things and did such wonderful things that people began to follow him. But they didn't know who he was. So one day they simply had to ask him. And he said, "I am . . . the Light."

When the word "light" is said, strike the match and light the Christ candle.

Let's enjoy the Light.

Sit peacefully and enjoy the light.

People who love the Light can become one with the Light. This is how your light became one with the Light. Watch.

Hold up one of the small candles and look at it. Then look at the child opposite you and say:

[Name], this is your light.

Light the child's candle from the Christ candle and place it in a candle holder on the white underlay in front of the Christ candle, opposite the child. You will continue lighting candles for the rest of the group, alternating to the left and right of the center child so a semicircle is formed around the Christ candle representative of where each child is sitting. [You need to start opposite you and place the candles from the center so you will not be burned while reaching over candles. WARNING: *You must be careful to reach around the Christ candle so you will not be burned or catch your clothing or hair on fire.]*

Now take another candle and hold it up toward the next child. Look at the child and say:

[Name], this is your light.

Light the candle, put it in a holder, and place it next to the first candle. Alternating from both sides of the center child, continue lighting candles for each child, placing them in holders, forming a semicircle around the Christ candle. When several candles are lit, say:

Look how the light is growing. It all came from the Light here.

Point to the Light.

Look, the light is in so many places at once.

After lighting more candles, say:

Many have come to the Light to receive their light. But the Light is not smaller. It is still the same. . . . I wonder how so much light could be given away and the Light still be the same?

When all the children have a candle lighted for them, light one for yourself and say:

There was even a day when I received my light and became one with the Light. . . . Let's enjoy the light.

Sit silently and enjoy the light.

There comes a time when the Light is changed so it's not just in one place anymore. It can be in many places at once. Watch. You see the light is just in one place now.

Point to the flame in your candle.

I'm going to change the light so it is not just in one place anymore. It can be in many places all at once. Watch.

Slowly lower the candle snuffer over your light, holding it over the wick a moment and then slowly raising it. Watch the smoke curl up into the air and fade into the whole room.

Now I will change each of your lights so they can be in more than one place.

Go around the circle and change the light of each child. When all the lights are changed, change the Light as you say:

Even the Light was changed. The Light that was just in one place at one time is in all places at all times. So the Light can be everywhere in this room and even in other places.

Sit silently for a moment and then slowly put all the materials back on the shelf.

I wonder if you would like to make something that shows how this story feels to you. You may use crayons, markers, or chalk. In just a moment I'll go around the circle and see what you would like to do.

Before you go to your work, let's remember what to do if you want to talk to me or need help. [Child's name], will you show us what to do if you need help or want to talk to me?

This is what I do if I want to talk to you.

Walk to the light switch, signal with the lights, and look at all the children's eyes. Then return to the circle.

Now I wonder what work you would like to do today? [Child's name], what would you like to do?

While the first child is getting a rug (or materials), ask the next child what he or she would like to do. Continue one at a time around the circle. Don't worry if this takes a long time. If they don't learn to do this now you will have confusion the rest of the year.

When it is time to get ready for the feast, use the light switch (or another signal). When you have their attention, say:

Now it is time to put your work away. You don't need to hurry. If you're not finished that's all right. You can put your work in your special folder. You can finish it the next time you're here. We don't lose children's work in this place.

Return to your place in the circle. The greeters will help if needed. As the children are putting their things away, reach behind you and take the liturgical cloth for the season. Spread it on the floor in front of you. Then place the Christ candle on it and then the Bible. Wait for the children to gather.

We Read the Bible

This is the Bible. Another way we listen to God is by reading the Bible. And we light the Christ candle to remind us that Jesus is still with us as we listen to the word of God.

Light the candle.

The story we heard today is in the Bible. Look.

Open the Bible to John 8:12 and turn it so the children can see the words that have been highlighted. Then read the words slowly.

I will put a marker in this place so you will know where this story is found. Look, there is a picture of a candle on the marker. You might want to look at these words yourself, or you might like someone to read them to you.

Slowly put the marker in the Bible, so the children can see, and place the Bible back on the cloth.

We Thank God

Now it is time to give thanks to God. You can say something you are thankful for or something about the story or your work today. You may talk to God out loud. Or if you don't want to talk out loud to God, that's all right too. God listens even if we don't speak out loud. We get ready to pray by saying:

L: Let us give thanks to the Lord our God.
C: It is right to give thanks and praise.
L: Let us pray.

Give sufficient time for praying. Be at home in the silence, giving the children time to pray. When the praying is over, say:

I am going to change the Light now. Look, the light is all in one place. I'm going to change the Light so it is not just in one place anymore. It can be in many places at once. Watch.

Change the Light as you did earlier. Then return the candle, then the Bible, and then the cloth to the shelf.

We Have a Feast

It is time to get ready for a feast. Let's get our legs ready. . . . Now let's get our tables ready.

When everyone has made a table, say:

Today our feast is [describe]. You may have one of each. Put them on your table like this and wait until everyone is served. Watch.

The greeter serves you first so you can demonstrate what to do. When all are served, say:

Thank you God for this joyful feast.
Let us enjoy the feast together.

Have a joyful time of conversation, and when all are finished, say:

Now let's put away our tables.

Silently take the paper cup off your napkin. Gather the four corners of the napkin together. Then put the napkin into the cup. Say:

Now [name] will come with the wastebasket for your cup.

We Go in God's Name

When it is time to go home, we have a special way to say good-bye. [Name of greeter] will come to you and say, " [Name] is here for you." I want to say good-bye to each of you and give you a blessing. So first come to me so we can say good-bye and I can bless you.

We can sing "Go Now in Peace" while we are waiting.

Each child comes to you and is touched and given a positive, personal word and then a benediction. This is done quietly so no one but the child hears. End by saying:

God go with you. Go in peace.

MATERIALS

1. White satin underlay, 24 by 36 inches
2. The Christ candle, a large white candle with a wide base, at least 3 by 9 inches
3. Tray with smaller white candles and candle holders, one for each child
4. Matches in a covered glass container
5. Candle snuffer
6. Marker with candle picture

Worship Center Order

PREPARATION FOR WORSHIP

Just as pastors and elders meet before the worship service for preparation and prayer, so the children's worship leader and greeters arrive early to make the final preparations of the room and the feast. The leader sits on the circle on the floor, praying and becoming centered in God in order to be ready when the first child arrives. The greeters are at the door to meet the children. Outside the door, the children prepare to enter this special place to be with God, to talk with God, and to hear the stories of God.

WE APPROACH GOD

The Greeting

Greet each child as he or she sits down on the circle. Talk with the children while the others arrive. When everyone is present, exchange a formal liturgical greeting that is appropriate for the season of the church year, such as (from September to Easter):

L: The Lord be with you.
C: And also with you.

or (from Easter to September):

L: Christ is risen.
C: The Lord is risen indeed.

Songs of Praise

Sing one or two songs of praise. Then end by singing and signing "Be Still and Know That I Am God."

WE PROCLAIM GOD'S WORD

Telling God's Word

When you have finished singing, say: When we sing these words, we know it is time to get ready to hear one of God's stories. So cross your legs and hug your hands or hug your knees, and watch closely where I go, so you will always know where the [name of materials] is kept.

> *Go to* **Part III, "Presentations."** *find the story or parable for the session, and insert it here.*

Responding to God's Word: Wondering Together

The wondering questions are at the end of each story. When you have finished wondering together, say:

> Watch closely how I put these materials away so they will be ready for the next person to use.

Place the materials back in the box in reverse order. Do it slowly, carefully. as though saying good-bye to good friends. Be silent, so the children will watch what you do. When you are finished, say:

> Watch closely where I go, so you will always know where these materials are kept. You might want to use them for your work today.

Walk silently and slowly to the shelf, carrying the materials carefully with both hands. Return silently to the circle. Remain centered.

Responding to God's Word: Story and Art Materials

Say in a quiet voice:

> I wonder if you would like to make something that shows how you feel about this story [or parable]. You could make this your work today. Or if there is other work you would like to get out, that's fine too. Perhaps you had work from last week you would like to do. We'll go around the circle now to see what you would like to do.

Ask the first child to your right what he or she would like to do. That child goes and gets those materials. Then ask the next child, and proceed around the circle until all are working. If a child doesn't know what to do, say:

> That's all right. Think a little longer, and I will come back to you.

Then come back to those who don't know and help them decide. Don't interrupt the children by approaching or talking to them. If they want help they will come to you. Exception: If the children misuse the materials, interrupt and retell the story so they will know how to use them.

Returning to the Circle

When the response time is almost over, signal with the lights (or use another signal; some leaders prefer to speak individually to each child). When you have the attention of the children, say:

Now it's time to get ready for the feast. You don't have to hurry. If you're not finished, that's all right. You can put your work in your special folder and finish it the next time you're here. We don't lose children's work in this place.

Return to your place in the circle so you are ready as the children gather in the circle again. The greeters help anyone who needs it. As the children are putting their things away, reach behind you and take a liturgical cloth for the season and spread it on the floor in front of you. Then place the Christ candle on it, the Bible, and the children's offerings.

Reading the Bible

When the children are seated on the circle, light the candle and say:

We light the Christ candle to remind us that Christ is with us as we hear the word of God.

Look at the Bible and then slowly trace the edges, saying:

This is the Bible. The story [parable] we heard today is in the Bible. Look.

Open the Bible to the passage for the day and turn it so the children can see the words that have been highlighted. Read the words slowly and meaningfully. Then say:

I will put a marker in this place so you will know where this story is found. Look. There is a picture of a _____ on it. You might want to look at these words yourself, or you might like someone to read them to you.

Slowly put the marker in the Bible, so the children can see, and place the Bible back on the cloth.

WE GIVE THANKS TO GOD

Prayer of Thanksgiving

Now it is time to give thanks to God. You can say something you are thankful for, or something about the story or your work today. You may talk to God out loud. Or if you don't want to talk out loud to God, that is all right too. God listens even if we don't speak out loud. . . . Let's get ready to pray.

Say and sign these words, which precede the Great Prayer of Thanksgiving:

L: Let us give thanks to the Lord our God.
C: It is right to give thanks and praise.
L: Let us pray.

Allow sufficient time for praying. Be at home in the silence, giving the children time to pray. When the praying is over, and before you extinguish the candle, say:

I am going to change the Light now.

Point to the flame (after the first few weeks, you may omit the spoken explanation):

Look, the Light is all in one place now. I'm going to change the Light so it is not just in one place anymore. It can be in many places at once. Watch.

Place the candle snuffer over the flame to catch the smoke as the flame goes out. Then slowly lift the snuffer and watch the smoke curl in the air and spread throughout the room. Then say:

Now the Light of Christ that was just in one place at one time is in all places in all times. So the Light can be everywhere in this room and even in other places.

Return the materials to the shelf.

Preparation of the Feast

Now it is time for the feast. This is how to make a table for the feast. Watch.

Take a large white paper napkin and place it in front of you on the floor. Silently and slowly, unfold it. Smooth it out with your hands. Then a child distributes napkins to the others.

Today our feast is [names of foods]. You may have [the amounts that each may take].

Two children distribute the food. One greeter carries the juice on a tray, while another offers a paper cup of juice to each person. Then say:

Thank you, God, for this joyous feast. Let us enjoy the feast together.

The Feast

Have a joyful time of conversation as you eat. When everyone has finished, say:

Now I will show you how to put away your table. Watch.

Take the cup off your napkin. Gather the four corners of the napkin together. Then put the napkin into the cup. Say:

Now [name of child] will come with the wastebasket for your cup.

GO IN GOD'S NAME

After the cups are collected, say:

When someone comes for you, [name of greeter] will come and tell you. I would like to say good-bye to you and give you a blessing. So first come to me so we can say good-bye and I can bless you.

Benediction

Sing together: "Go Now in Peace." Each child goes to the leader, is touched, and is given a positive, personal word that affirms his or her gifts for ministry. Do this quietly so no one but the child hears. Then say a blessing, a benediction—a sign that the power of God goes with us as we go in God's name to minister in the world. Say:

The love of God go with you. Go in peace.

PART III

PRESENTATIONS

5

The Good Shepherd
Psalm 23

*Walk slowly to the parable shelf and pick up the **Good Shepherd** box. Carry it to the circle. Put the box down in front of you and look at it. Take a moment of silence to center yourself. Touch the box gently, with wonder, and say:*

I wonder if this is a parable? Hmm. It might be. Parables are very precious, like gold, and this box is gold.

Gently run your hand over the lid.

This looks like a present.

Lift the box and admire it like a present.

Well, parables are like presents. They have already been given to us. We can't buy them, or take them, or steal them. They are already ours. . . . There's another reason why this might be a parable. It has a lid.

Trace the lid of the box with your fingers.

And sometimes parables seem to have lids on them. But when you lift the lid of a parable there is something very precious inside. . . . I know. Let's take off the lid and see if this is a parable.

Lift the lid and peek inside. Put the lid back on and move the box to your side. Then open the lid just enough to take out the materials but not enough for the children to see inside. Take out the green underlay with wonder and say:

I wonder what this could be?

Begin smoothing out the underlay and say:

It's so green. It's so soft and warm. I wonder what could be so green?

As the children respond, incorporate their responses into the story. (Don't discuss them.) For example:

CHILDREN

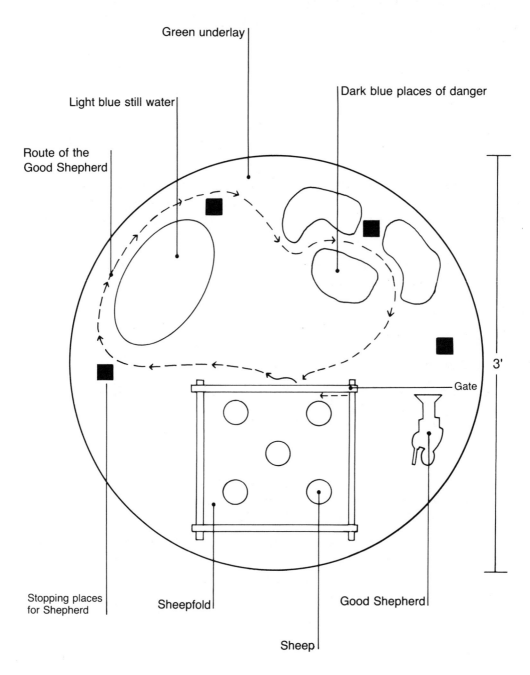

Green underlay

Dark blue places of danger

Light blue still water

Route of the
Good Shepherd

3'

Gate

Stopping places
for Shepherd

Sheepfold

Good Shepherd

Sheep

LEADER

Yes, it could be grass . . . or a bush . . . or a tree . . . or a balloon. . . . Perhaps it is a large green meadow.

Sit back and reflect a moment.

Maybe there is something else that will help us.

Take out the light blue felt. Present it, saying:

Yes. There is this.

Place it on the underlay to your upper left and smooth it out slowly.

It's so blue . . . and cool. I wonder what it might be?

Again, incorporate the responses into your story. For example:

Yes, it could be water. . . . Perhaps it is a piece of the sky . . . or a mirror . . . or a window to see through to the other side. Let's see if there's anything else.

Look into the box and take out the dark blue pieces of felt. Present them.

These are very dark. There seems to be no light in them at all.

Place the dark blue pieces on the upper right corner from you, spaced so the Good Shepherd can lead the sheep through.

I wonder what these could be? . . . I wonder if there is more?

Take out a tan strip from the box.

I wonder what this could be? If I place it here . . .

Place it horizontally near the edge of the circle closest to you and smooth it out.

. . . it looks like a road.

Walk your fingers from one end of the strip to the other, saying:

This could be the beginning, and this could be the end. Or this could be the beginning and this the end.

Bring out another strip and place it parallel.

If I add another . . . then the road could be in between.

Glide your hand between the strips.

Then this could be the beginning and this the end. Or this might be the beginning and this the end.

Place two more strips to make a square and continue laying the remaining eight strips on the first four, as you say:

There are more. If I put one here, and one here . . . I could make this place very strong. It's getting stronger . . . and stronger. Now I wonder what this could be? It could be a log cabin. . . . Hmm, it could be a corral.

Point to the inside of the sheepfold and then to the outside.

There is an inside . . . and an outside in this place. But I think there needs to be a way to go out . . . and a way to come in. . . . I could make a gate.

Make a gate by separating the ends of the strips in the corner farthest from you at your right.

I wonder who lives here?

Look into the box and take out the sheep.

Here are some sheep. If sheep live in this place, then it must be a sheepfold. It is called a sheepfold because the sheep are folded safely inside.

Trace the sheepfold with your finger. Sit back, pondering for a moment, remaining centered and looking at the material. Be sure to keep your eyes on the material during the telling of the story. You do not want to break the story with eye contact. Continue:

Once there was someone who said such amazing things and did such wonderful things that people began to follow him. But they didn't know who he was. So one day they simply had to ask him, and he said . . .

Take the Good Shepherd figure from the box, present it, and place it on the underlay as you say:

"I am the Good Shepherd. I know each one of my sheep by name.

Touch each of the sheep in the sheepfold.

And they know the sound of my voice. So when I call my sheep from the sheepfold, they follow me.

Open the gate.

I walk in front of the sheep to show them the way.

Slide the Good Shepherd out into the open "grass" at the left of the underlay. Slide the sheep one at a time as they follow the Good Shepherd.

I show them the way to the good green grass. . . . I show them the way to the cool, clear, still water. . . .

Slide all the sheep so they are around the blue felt pond, drinking.

And when there are places of danger . . .

Slide the Good Shepherd to the dark blue "rocks." Then move the sheep one at a time.

. . . I show them the way to pass through. . . .

Slide the Good Shepherd through the rocks. Then move the sheep through the places of danger. Then move them into the sheepfold.

. . . so they can come safely home to the sheepfold."

Close the gate. Pause. Sit back.

Responding to God's Word: Wondering Together

Begin wondering with the children.

I wonder if the sheep have names? . . .

I wonder if the sheep are happy in this place? . . .

Trace the sheepfold with your fingers.

I wonder how many sheep really could live in this place? . . .

I wonder if you have ever had to go through places of danger? . . .

I wonder how the sheep feel with the Good Shepherd? . . .

I wonder how the Good Shepherd feels about the sheep? . . .

Trace the sheepfold with your fingers.

I wonder where this place might really be? . . .

Trace the outline of the whole underlay.

I wonder where this whole place might really be? . . .

Return to the weekly worship center order and continue. The scripture reading is Psalm 23:1–4.

MATERIALS

1. Gold parable box (a business-size envelope box wrapped in gold paper)
2. Green felt cut into a circle 36 inches in diameter
3. Light blue felt cut into an oval pond about 8 by 11 inches
4. Three pieces of dark blue felt about 4 by 5 inches each cut into irregularly shaped pieces to represent rocks
5. Twelve strips of tan felt 1 by 14 inches
6. *Five multicolored sheep, laminated
7. *Good Shepherd, laminated
8. *Ordinary shepherd, laminated for Session 39
9. *Wolf, laminated for Session 39

---

*Patterns and instructions for items marked with an asterisk, here and throughout, appear in Part IV.

6

The Good Shepherd
and the Lost Sheep
Psalm 23 and John 10

For this session, repeat the actions and words of Session 5, **The Good Shepherd,** *to the point where the shepherd moves safely through the rocks. Then, as you move the sheep through, pick up as follows:*

Move the sheep after the Good Shepherd, losing one in the rocks.

"I count each of my sheep as they go inside.

Point silently to each sheep. Pause and point to the empty space.

And if one is missing, I would go anywhere to look for the lost sheep . . .

Slowly move the Good Shepherd through the grass, by the water, and stop in the rocks.

. . . through the green grass . . . by the still water . . . calling my sheep by name, even in places of danger. And when I find the lost sheep, I carry it home . . .

Place missing sheep on the Good Shepherd and continue moving through the places of danger.

. . . even if it is very heavy . . . even if I am very tired.

Place the sheep in the sheepfold and close the gate.

When all my sheep are safe inside, I'm so happy. . . . But I can't be happy all by myself, so I call all my friends, and we have a great feast."

Pause. Move the Good Shepherd back alongside the sheepfold.

Responding to God's Word: Wondering Together

Begin wondering with the children.

   I wonder if these sheep have names? . . .

   I wonder if the sheep are happy in this place? . . .

Trace the sheepfold with your finger.

   I wonder how many sheep really could live in this place? . . .

   I wonder if you have ever had to go through places of danger or were lost and someone found you? . . .

   I wonder if you have ever heard the Good Shepherd say your name? . . .

   I wonder who these sheep might really be? . . .

   I wonder who the Good Shepherd might really be? . . .

   I wonder how the Good Shepherd feels about the sheep? . . .

Trace the shape of the sheepfold.

   I wonder where this place might really be? . . .

Trace the outline of the whole underlay.

   I wonder where this whole place might really be? . . .

Return to the weekly worship center order and continue. The scripture reading is Luke 15:3–6.

7

Creation
Genesis 1:1–2:3

*Walk slowly to the sacred story shelf and pick up the tray with the **Creation** materials. Carry it carefully with two hands to the circle and place it beside you. Sit quietly while you feel the story forming in you. Then say:*

What are some of the biggest gifts you have?

Listen to the responses and value each one, but say:

That is a very big gift, but think of something even bigger. There are some gifts that are so big that it's very hard to see them. They're everywhere, but they are so big we forget they are here. I don't know how to see them unless we go back to the beginning . . . or just before the beginning. Let's see if we can do that.

Slowly unroll the dark blue felt underlay and smooth it out.

In the beginning there was nothing . . . except God . . . and perhaps an enormmous smile.

Trace an invisible smile with your finger running the length of the underlay.

On the first day God gave us the gift of light.

Pick up the card with darkness and light, present it, and place it on the underlay. Touch the light.

I don't mean "light" like the light in this room or the light you can turn on and off. I don't mean the light of the sun, moon, and stars. I mean **light**. All light. What is present in light that makes it light. . . . When God saw the light, God said, "It is good."

Touch the light and raise your hand above it as though blessing it.

On the second day God gave us the gift of water.

Pick up the card with the firmament, present it, and put it next to the first card. Touch the water.

I don't just mean the water in a glass or the water in the bathtub, or the water that comes from the sky. I mean **water**. All water. What is present in water that makes it water. . . . When God saw the water, God said, "It is good."

Touch the water and raise your hand above it as though blessing it.

On the third day God gave us the gift of the dry land . . .

Present and put down the card with water, land, and growing things, and point to the land.

. . . and the growing things.

Point to the growing things.

I mean all the **land** and all the **green growing things**. . . . And when God saw the dry land and the green growing things, God said, "They are good."

Touch the dry land and the growing things and bless them.

On the fourth day God gave us the gift of the great lights.

Present and put down the card with the sun, moon, and stars.

The great light that rules the day . . .

Touch the sun.

. . . and the great light that rules the night.

Touch the moon.

And when God saw the great lights, God said, "They are good."

Touch the great lights and bless them.

On the fifth day God gave us the gift of the fish that swim in the sea and the birds that fly in the air.

Present and put down the card with the fish and birds. Touch the fish and birds.

When God saw the fish and the birds, God said, "They are good."

Touch the fish and the birds, and bless them.

On the sixth day God gave us the gift of the creatures that walk upon the earth: the animals and the people.

Present and put down the card with the animals and people. Point to them.

When God saw the animals and the people, God said, "They are good."

Touch the animals and people, and bless them. Pause. Then slowly move your hand over all the cards with a blessing motion as you say:

And God saw everything that was made, and God said, "It is very good."

On the seventh day God gave us the gift of a day to rest and remember the gifts of all the other days.

Present and put down the white seventh card and move your hand back over all the cards.

On this day we find a special place to remember all the gifts of God.

Responding to God's Word: Wondering Together

I wonder what special place you would go to remember God's gifts of Creation?

Let the children name their special places.

You can make a set of these cards to remember the gifts of Creation. When you make your cards you can make a picture of your special place for remembering the gifts of God on this white card. When you are working with this material, remember there is something that can help you. Look.

Pick up the cards that are bound together and unfold them above the cards you first laid out.

This can show you which gift comes after which in all the gifts of Creation.

If this is the first time the children will be tearing or cutting and pasting, demonstrate how.

Return to the weekly worship center order and continue. The scripture reading is Genesis 1:1–5.

MATERIALS

1. *Two sets of seven laminated 6-by-8-inch Creation cards, one set attached in a strip and the other set laminated separately
2. Rectangle of dark blue felt, 15 by 72 inches
3. Seven baskets 2 to 2½ inches, for materials
4. Construction paper for children to make their own cards: yellow, dark blue, royal blue, white, light blue, green, and brown
5. Moons, suns, and stars, enough for each child to paste (older children can cut their own)
6. Tray for Creation cards and felt
7. Clear file trays for cut-out figures for pasting

Card One
Darkness and Light

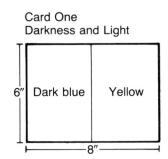

Card Two
Firmament and Water

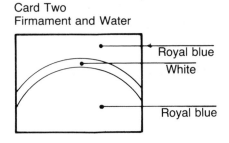

Card Three
Land and Growing Things

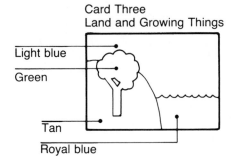

Card Four
The Great Lights

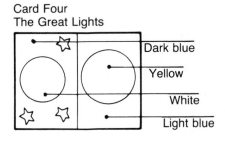

Card Five
Fish and Birds

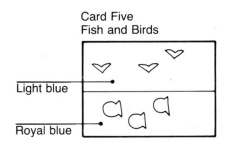

Card Six
Animals and People

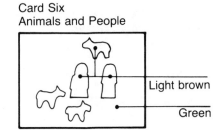

Card Seven

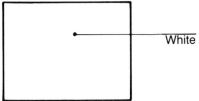

8

Noah
Genesis 6:9–9:29

Walk slowly to the sacred story shelf and pick up the tray with the **Noah** *materials. Carry it carefully with two hands to the circle and place it beside you. Sit quietly while you feel the story forming in you. Then roll out the dark blue underlay and smooth it out as you say:*

In the beginning God gave us our biggest gifts, the gifts of light and water, earth and people. And God said, "They are very good." But the people grew wicked and did bad things.

Move your hands above the underlay. Clench your fists. Twist your hands together, making violent gestures.

God was very sad. Everything that was good and clean and new at creation seemed spoiled. But there was one good family. There was the mother and the father Noah.

Present Mr. and Mrs. Noah and place them on the underlay.

God said to Noah, "I will send a great flood of water to wash everything clean and to make it new again. Build an ark . . .

Place the ark on the underlay.

. . . and place every kind of animal family in the ark."

The animals came from everywhere.

Set out the animals in twos in a semicircle around the ark. Don't name them. Silently and with ceremony move them into the ark. Noah and his wife go in last. Make sure they are very secure in the ark.

It began to rain . . .

Lift up your arms and let your hands bring down the rain. Do this three times as you say:

. . . and rain . . . and rain. It rained for forty days and forty nights.

Begin to lift the ark, rocking it back and forth as the water level rises. The ark goes up over the heads of the children and finally over your head.

All the earth and everyone and everything on it was covered with water. But not the ark. . . . God remembered Noah. The rain stopped.

Continue holding the ark over everyone's head.

God sent a wind to dry up the water.

Silently bring the ark down (as the water level lowers) until it rests on the underlay again.

One day Noah took a dove . . .

Pick up the dove, place it on the palm of your hand, and say:

. . . and held out his hand, and the dove flew off.

Fly the dove off with your other hand.

It found only water. So it returned.

Fly the dove back and receive it with care.

Noah sent the dove a second time. It returned with an olive leaf.

Send out and receive the dove as above with a piece of green leaf it picked up.

Noah sent the dove a third time. The dove did not return. It had a new home.

This time get up while you are talking and fly the dove over to the window, where you hook it to a blue ribbon you have hung there. This ribbon remains in the room so the children can also use it when they use this material.

All the animals came out of the ark. They were home too.

Bring the animals out and set them in pairs, radiating out from the ark like spokes from the hub of a wheel.

Everything was clean and new again. Noah and his family were so happy they couldn't help but give thanks to God. So they built a special place . . .

Build an altar.

. . . an altar, and prayed their thanksgiving, for they were home. And God promised never to send such a flood of water again. God gave a sign, a rainbow . . .

Make the shape of a bow in the sky over the ark and the creatures.

. . . so we can always remember God's promise. We can still see the rainbow in the sky. It was the sign for Noah and it is the sign for us too: that there will never be such a flood again. Now we can't have the whole rainbow in our center, but we can have a piece of the rainbow. When you work with this . . .

Hold up the prism and turn it to see the "rainbow."

. . . you look in here very carefully and you will see a piece of the rainbow. Just turn it.

Responding to God's Word: Wondering Together

I wonder how it felt to be in the ark in all that rain? . . .

I wonder what it was like to be surrounded by so much water? . . .

I wonder how it felt to be washed clean and new and to start all over again? . . .

I wonder how God felt about the animals and people in the ark? . . .

Touch the altar.

I wonder how they felt as they made a special place to talk to God, to say their thanks to God? . . .

I wonder how they felt when they saw the rainbow? . . .

Return to the weekly worship center order and continue. The scripture reading is Genesis 9:8–15.

MATERIALS

1. Rectangle of dark blue felt, 24 by 36 inches
2. Noah's Ark*
3. Five pairs of animals
4. Basket for animals (7-inch)
5. Noah and wife figures
6. Dove
7. Small stones for altar
8. Three 4-inch baskets, for Noahs, dove, and stones
9. Prism
10. Small flashlight
11. Basket or box for prism and flashlight, 2 by 4 inches

---

*Local stores sell Noah's Arks with animals or you can make your own. An all-wood ark over 18 inches long with 26 pieces can be ordered from Lillian Vernon Corp., 510 South Fulton Avenue, Mount Vernon, NY 10550 for under $25.

12. Thread of green yarn (or ribbon) for olive branch
13. Tray for above items
14. Blue ribbon to hang at window before session begins

CHILDREN

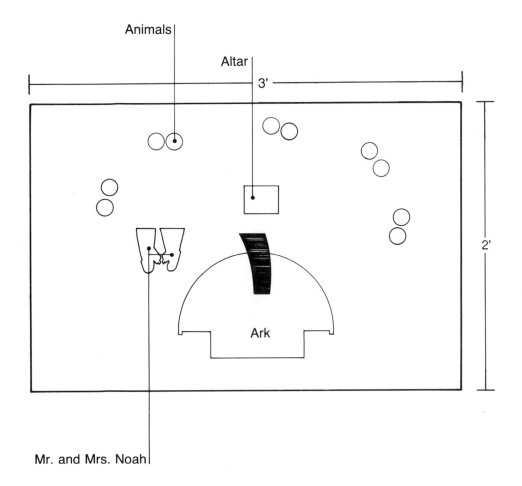

Animals

Altar

3'

2'

Ark

Mr. and Mrs. Noah

LEADER

9

Abram and Sarai
Genesis 12 and 13

Walk slowly to the desert box and move it to the circle. Return to the sacred story shelf to get the tray with the **Abram and Sarai** *materials. Carry it carefully with two hands to the circle and place it beside you. Sit quietly while you feel the story forming in you. Then say:*

This is the desert box.

Trace the edge of the desert box.

Inside is a small piece of the desert. . . . So many important things happen in the desert that we just have to have a small piece of it in our room.

Slowly move your hands over the sand, smoothing and molding it, as the sand is transformed into the desert.

The desert is a strange and wild place. At night it is very cold, but in the day it is burning hot. There is almost no water at all. . . . The desert is always changing. The wind comes. And as it blows it shapes and molds. So the desert is never the same.

Pause, place your hands in your lap, and sit back a moment. Then say:

Once Abram . . .

Place Abram in the desert box near the edge closest to you.

. . . and Sarai . . .

Place Sarai next to Abram.

. . . lived in the beautiful city of Haran.

Place Haran to the left of Abram and Sarai.

The one true God loved Abram and Sarai.

Move them a little bit from Haran.

One day God said to them, "Move from your home. I will give you a new home and a new land. It's all right to go. I will be with you. And I will bless you . . .

Place your hand on their heads as a blessing.

. . . and I will make you a blessing."

Abram and Sarai looked across the desert. It would be sad to leave their home and their friends.

Move your hand slowly across the desert.

They wondered if they would be safe. Would God be with them?

Move your hand across the desert and hesitate in several places.

Abram and Sarai went. They trusted the one true God to show them the way.

Move them toward your right, along the edge nearest you. Then begin moving them away from you toward the children at the other side of the box as if they were moving into Canaan.

They came to Shechem in the land of Canaan. God had been with them in Haran.

Touch Haran.

But would God be here too?

Touch imaginary Shechem.

Then God said to them, "Look. Look at all this land. . . .

Move your hand above Canaan.

. . . I will give this land to your children." Abram and Sarai were so happy that God was with them, they couldn't help but give thanks to God. So they built a special place, an altar and prayed their thanks to God.

Build an altar with stones.

Then they moved on to a place near Bethel.

Move them near imaginary Bethel.

And God was there too. Abram and Sarai were so happy that God was with them, they couldn't help but give thanks to God. So they built an altar and prayed their thanks.

Build another altar.

Then there came a great famine so there was not enough food to eat. They were very hungry. So Abram and Sarai moved to the land of Egypt for food.

Move them to the corner of the desert box.

Abram was scared. He was scared of the people in Egypt. He forgot that God had promised to be with him. But God did not forget. God kept

Abram and Sarai safe. The Egyptians were good to them, and gave them food and animals. . . . Abram and Sarai moved back to the land of Canaan, the land God promised to give them, to a place called Hebron.

Move them to imaginary Hebron.

Abram and Sarai wondered if God would be here too. God had been with them in Haran . . .

Point to each place.

. . . and in Shechem, and near Bethel, and in Egypt. Would God be in Hebron too? Then God said to them, "I will give you many children to live in this land." Abram and Sarai were so happy that God was with them, they couldn't help but give thanks to God. So they built an altar and prayed their thanks . . .

Make an altar.

. . . to the one true God who was with them.

Gesture a blessing over them.

Now Abram and Sarai knew that the one true God who spoke to them and showed them the way . . .

Trace the journey with your finger in the sand.

. . . was in every place . . .

Point to each place.

. . . and in every time . . . just as God promised.

Pause and sit back.

Responding to God's Word: Wondering Together

I wonder how Abram and Sarai felt when they were told to move to a new home? . . .

I wonder how it felt to leave their home and not know where they were going?

Motion around the desert.

I wonder if you have ever gone somewhere and didn't know where you were going? . . .

Move your hand through the desert.

I wonder how Abram and Sarai felt going through the desert looking for a place to live? . . .

Touch each place.

I wonder how they felt when God spoke to them in all these places?

Move your hand back and forth between the places.

I wonder what God was doing when Abram and Sarai were traveling between these places? . . .

I wonder where God is when you go from place to place? . . .

I wonder how many places God can be? . . .

Return to the weekly worship center order and continue. The scripture reading is Genesis 12:1–4a.

MATERIALS

1. Desert box, wood or plastic, 24" × 36" × 4" deep, filled with clean sand*
2. *Abram and Sarai figures
3. Stones to make three altars
4. Two small baskets, 4-inch for figures, 5-inch for stones
5. Small city of Haran, made of foam board or small wood blocks glued side by side
6. Tray for materials

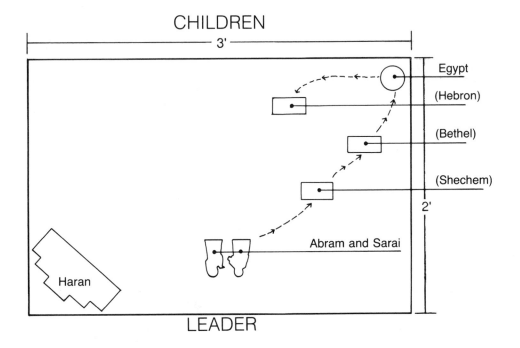

---

*You may want to refer to a map of Canaan for help in moving the figures.

10

Exodus
Exodus 1:1–15:21

Walk slowly to the desert box and move it to the circle. Return to the sacred story shelf to get the tray with the **Exodus** *materials. Carry it carefully with two hands to the circle and place it beside you. Sit quietly while you feel the story forming in you. Then say:*

This is the desert box.

Trace the edge of the desert box.

Inside is a small piece of the desert. . . . So many important things happen in the desert that we just have to have a small piece of it in our room.

Slowly move your hands over the sand, smoothing and molding it as the sand is transformed into the desert.

The desert is a strange and wild place. At night it is very cold, but in the day it is burning hot. There is almost no water at all. . . . The desert is always changing. The wind comes. And as it blows it shapes and molds. So the desert is never the same.

Pause, place your hands in your lap, and sit back a moment.

Once the children were very hungry.

Place some figures of children lying down in the sand in the left-hand corner of the box nearest you.

They cried in the night, even when they were asleep. Their parents heard them . . .

Place the parents around them.

. . . but there was no food. They knew they had to find food, so the people of God crossed the desert to the land of Egypt.

Move the people across the desert to Egypt (the far right-hand corner).

They stayed. But one day a new king, called a pharaoh, wanted the people of God for slaves. Pharaoh caught them in a trap.

Cup both hands over the people as though you were trapping them.

He would not let them go. The people of God had do what Pharaoh said. They had to work when Pharaoh said. They had to live where Pharaoh said. They had to go to bed when Pharaoh said. They couldn't do anything on their own.

The people of God cried to God for help, and God heard them. God spoke to Moses . . .

Present Moses and place him at a distance. Then move him toward imaginary Pharaoh.

. . . and said, "Go to Pharaoh and say, 'Let God's people go!' " But Pharaoh said, "No."

Sit back, fold your arms, and look as if the matter is settled. Move Moses back to the people.

Many terrible things happened in the land of Egypt. But still Pharaoh said, "No." Finally, the firstborn of all the Egyptian families and animals died. But not the people of God. They were safe. Death passed over them.

Cup your hand over the people. Move Moses back to Pharaoh.

Moses went to Pharaoh again. And Pharaoh said, "Yes." Moses rushed back to the people.

Rush Moses back and speed up your voice by running together the following sentences:

The people of God were ready. They had to hurry before Pharaoh changed his mind. So they took unleavened bread because there wasn't time for it to rise.

Move the people.

They moved toward the great sea . . .

Take out the blue sea strips and place them in the middle of the box.

. . . fearing any moment they would hear the sound of Pharaoh's army chasing them to bring them back.

Move the people to the water. Press them up against the water's edge.

Then they heard the war chariots. Pharaoh's army was coming! They were pressed against the water, trapped again. Moses cried to God, and God showed Moses the way . . .

Fold the two strips back from the center and move Moses through.

> . . . the way *through* the water to freedom.

Move others through as you say:

> Look at the people of God. They are doing different things to show how they feel. I wonder if you would like to go through to freedom? When it's your turn you can come here and choose one of the people to take through.

Go around the circle. When each child has brought a person through, bring the rest through.

> When all the people of God passed through, the water closed . . .

Close the water.

> . . . and they were safe. They were free. The people of God were so happy they were free, they just had to thank the one true God. So they sang their thanks, and Miriam, the prophet, led the dancing.

Place the people in small groups in circles as if dancing. Pause.

Responding to God's Word: Wondering Together

> Now I wonder how it feels to be hungry and not have any food? . . .

> I wonder how the parents felt when they didn't have any food to give their children? . . .

> I wonder how it feels if the only way to get food is to be a slave? . . .

> I wonder if you have ever been near a place like this, trapped, and someone freed you? . . .

> I wonder how they felt when the firstborn of the Egyptians died but death passed over the people of God? . . .

> I wonder how it felt to be trapped again? . . .

Touch the sea.

> I wonder how it felt when God led them through the water to freedom? . . .

> Now that the people of God are free, I wonder which way they will go? . . .

> I wonder how they will know the way? . . .

Return to the weekly worship center order and continue. The scripture reading is Exodus 15:1–2.

MATERIALS

1. Desert box
2. *People of God, one for each child plus six extra
3. *Moses and Miriam
4. Basket for figures (5-inch)
5. Two strips of dark blue felt, each 24 inches long and 6 inches wide
6. Tray for materials

CHILDREN

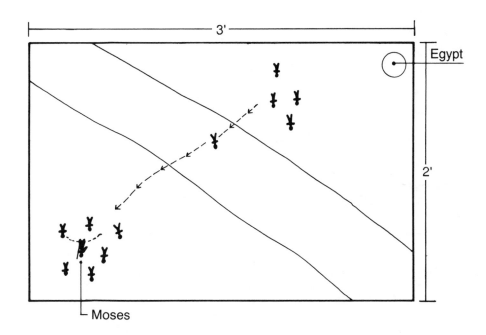

LEADER

11

The Ten Best Ways to Live
Exodus 19–20; Deuteronomy 6:4–6

Walk slowly to the desert box and move it to the circle. Return to the sacred story shelf to get the tray with the **Ten Best Ways to Live** *materials. Carry it carefully with two hands to the circle and place it beside you. Return to the shelf for Mount Sinai and place it beside you. Sit quietly while you feel the story forming in you. Then say:*

This is the desert box.

Trace the edge of the desert box.

Inside is a small piece of the desert. . . . So many important things happen in the desert that we just have to have a small piece of it in our room.

Slowly move your hands over the sand, smoothing and molding it as the sand is transformed into the desert.

The desert is a strange and wild place. At night it is very cold, but in the day it is burning hot. There is almost no water at all. . . . The desert is always changing. The wind comes. And as it blows it shapes and molds. So the desert is never the same.

Pause, place your hands in your lap, and sit back a moment. Then begin putting people in the sand in the left corner of the desert box near the children as you say:

After God led the people of God through the water to freedom, they were free to go any way they wanted. But what was the best way to go? Well, God loved the people so much that God said to Moses:

Move Moses out in front.

"I will show you the way. I will lead you to the holy mountain, Mount Sinai."

Place Mount Sinai in the box in the left-hand corner near you. Move the people to the left, toward the mountain.

Now when they came close to the holy mountain they could see fire and smoke and they were afraid even to come close. But Moses went close.

Move Moses up the mountain.

Moses climbed the holy mountain and stayed there talking with God. And God told Moses the Ten Best Ways to Live.

Stand Moses on the top of the mountain for a few moments in silence and then bring him down to the base of the mountain and the people.

When Moses came down from the holy mountain, he gave the Ten Best Ways to Live to the people. There were four best ways for loving God.

Take the first tablet from the heart box and place it near Moses. Place the first four numbered tablet cards directly behind the tablet, but don't read them.

And there were six best ways for loving people.

Place the second tablet in the sand and add the last six numbered tablet cards directly behind it, but don't read them.

The Ten Best Ways to Live are so important we call them "the Law."

Lay the first tablets down on the sand, forming a heart. Then present and add the tip to complete the heart as you say:

We add this other piece so we can remember why God gave us the Law, the Ten Best Ways to Live. It says, "God loves you."

Responding to God's Word: Wondering Together

I wonder how it feels to be free, to be able to do anything you want to? . . .

I wonder how it feels to be able to do anything you want, but you don't know what to do? . . .

I wonder if it's hard to be free? . . .

I wonder how Moses felt going up the holy mountain? . . .

I wonder what Moses and God talked about? . . .

I wonder if it's hard to love God and love people? . . .

If you are working with children over seven years old you might wish to add the following, before the wondering questions.

Would you like to know what the Ten Best Ways to Live are that God told Moses? I can show you. The first are the best ways for loving God.

Hold up the first numbered tablet.

At the very beginning God said, "I am the one true God." This is very important. Everything depends on this. So the first commandment is, "Do not serve other gods."

Place the first tablet back in the sand. Hold up the others, one by one, as you name them.

The second is, "Make no idols to serve."

The third is, "I am God . . . so do not speak my name lightly."

"Keep the Sabbath holy . . . to rest and remember the gifts of creation."

The best ways to love people are:

"Honor your father and mother."

"Do not kill."

"Do not break your marriage."

"Do not steal."

"Do not lie."

"Do not even want what others have."

This is the Law. And it is hard. It is very hard to do what it says all the time, but God loves us and shows us the way to be the best people we can be. Now I wonder which is the most important to you?

Return to the weekly worship center order and continue. The scripture reading is Deuteronomy 6:4–6.

MATERIALS

1. Desert box
2. Large rock for Mount Sinai (10 to 12 inches wide, 6 or 7 inches high, 6 to 8 inches thick)
3. *People of God
4. *Moses
5. Basket for figures (5-inch)
6. *Two tablets cut from white poster board and laminated. On one, print the words LOVE GOD, using a white backing; on the other, LOVE PEOPLE, using a green backing.
7. *One triangular piece of posterboard, also laminated, to form the bottom of the heart shape. On it print the words GOD LOVES YOU.

8. *Ten individual tablets cut from white poster board, with Ten Commandments written as below. Use white backing for the first four and green backing for the remaining six.

1. Do not serve other gods
2. Make no idols to serve
3. Do not speak my name lightly
4. Keep the Sabbath holy
5. Honor your father and mother

6. Do not kill
7. Do not break your marriage
8. Do not steal
9. Do not lie
10. Do not want what others have

9. Two red heart-shaped boxes or baskets, one to contain the tablets (7 by 8 inches) and one for stickers for the children

CHILDREN

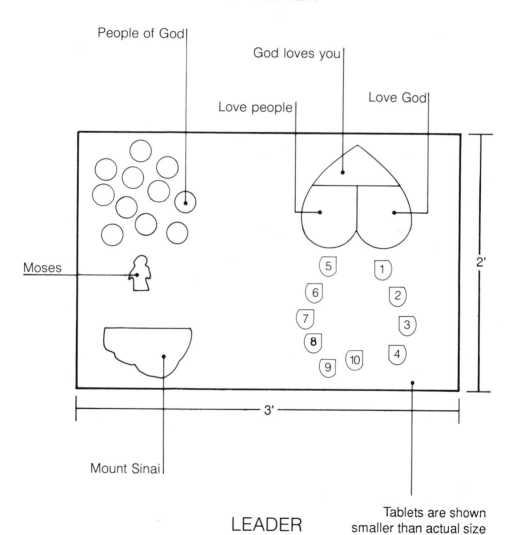

Tablets are shown smaller than actual size

LEADER

12

The Ark and a Tent for God
Exodus 25:1–40:38

Walk slowly to the desert box and move it to the circle. Return to the sacred story shelf to get the tray with the **Ark** *materials. Carry it carefully with two hands to the circle and place it beside you. Sit quietly while you feel the story forming in you. Then say:*

This is the desert box.

Trace the edge of the desert box.

Inside is a small piece of the desert. . . . So many important things happen in the desert that we just have to have a small piece of it in our room.

Slowly move your hands over the sand, smoothing and molding it as the sand is transformed into the desert.

The desert is a strange and wild place. At night it is very cold, but in the day it is burning hot. There is almost no water at all. . . . The desert is always changing. The wind comes. And as it blows it shapes and molds. So the desert is never the same.

Pause, place your hands in your lap, and sit back a moment.

God led the people through the waters to freedom and gave them the Ten Best Ways to Live. Now the people of God were on the way to the Promised Land, the land God promised to give them. The people of God loved the Ten Best Ways to Live so much that they wanted to carry them with them. But they needed a way to come close to something so precious. So God told them how.

First they made a special box, an Ark, to carry the Ten Best Ways to Live.

Present the Ark by placing it in the palm of your hand and touching with your finger each of the parts named. Do this with each piece that follows.

It was covered with gold, and on the top were two golden angels. And inside they put the Ten Best Ways to Live.

Place the Ark in the desert box at the west end facing east.

But now they needed a way to get ready to come close to the Ark.

Move the figure of a priest toward the Ark and then turn away and shrug shoulders.

So they made an altar where they could burn incense . . .

Present the Altar of Incense, point to it, and lift fingers, following the smoke. Place it in front of the Ark, leaving room for the veil.

. . . which made a wonderful smell and smoke. Now the priest . . .

Move the priest past the altar and around behind the Ark.

. . . could go through the sweet-smelling incense and smoke to the Ark and be close to God. But this still wasn't enough to come close to something so precious. So they made a special table called the Table of Shewbread.

Present, touch, and place the Table of Shewbread on the north side.

It was covered with gold, and every Sabbath day they put twelve loaves of unleavened bread on it. On the other side they put the gold candlestick with seven burning lights called the Menorah.

Present, touch, and place the Menorah opposite the Shewbread on the south.

Now the priest could walk between the Table of Shewbread and the Menorah through the sweet-smelling incense and smoke to the Ark and be close to God.

Walk the priest through.

But this still wasn't enough to get ready. So they made a tent, called a Tabernacle. Inside the Tabernacle, the tent for God, was a special veil that divided the inside room from the outside room. They called the inside room the Holy of Holies. And that's where they kept the Ark.

Present the Tabernacle, point to the veil, and trace the room with your finger. Then place it so the Ark is in the Holy of Holies. The opening of the Tabernacle faces east.

And now the priest could walk into the tent, between the Table of Shewbread and the Menorah, through the sweet-smelling incense and smoke, through the curtain, into the Holy of Holies to the Ark, and be close to God.

Walk the priest through.

Outside the tent for God, the people made sacrifices, at the great Altar of Burnt Offering.

Present, touch, and place the Altar of Burnt Offering outside the door, leaving room for the Laver.

Here they gave the very best of their animals to God. A great bowl of water, called the Laver . . .

Present, touch, and place the Laver in front of the door.

. . . was placed in front of the tent so the priests could wash their hands and feet before they went inside the tent, between the Table of Shewbread and the Menorah, through the sweet-smelling incense and smoke, through the curtain, into the Holy of Holies to the Ark, and be close to God.

Move the priest through.

They covered the tent for God with beautiful cloths.

Present, feel, and place the tent coverings one at a time.

And finally on the outside they put one that was rough and wooly, so when people passed by in the desert, they would see that and just pass on by.

Move your hand in the sand by the Tabernacle.

This was still not enough. They couldn't just leave all this sitting out in the desert, so they put a linen fence around it.

Put the fence around it.

Now they had a special place . . . and a special way to come near to God.

Pause a moment.

It was a tent for God. So whenever the people of God moved in the desert, they could take down the fence . . .

Pick up the tent and place it back on the tray. Continue with the rest until only the Ark is left.

. . . and the tent . . . and everything in it . . . and carry it with them. And the Ark . . .

Touch the Ark and move it forward in the sand leading the way.

. . . with the Ten Best Ways to Live led the way.

Responding to God's Word: Wondering Together

I wonder how it feels to come close to something so precious as the Ark? . . .

I wonder how the sweet-smelling incense and smoke helped them get ready to come near the Ark and close to God? . . .

I wonder how the Table of Shewbread with the unleavened bread helped them get ready to be close to God? . . .

I wonder how the great burning lights helped them get ready to be close to God? . . .

I wonder how you get ready to be close to God? . . .

I wonder how it feels to be close to God? . . .

I wonder where the Ten Best Ways to Live are now?

Pick up the Ark.

As the people of God journeyed through the desert toward the Promised Land, the Ark led the way. But the people of God do not carry the Ten Best Ways to Live in the Ark anymore.

Put the Ark back and pick up the heart box with the heart stickers in it.

Today we can carry the love for God and the love for people in our hearts.

Go around the circle and say each child's name as you attach a heart sticker to them and say:

[Name of child], you can have the love for God and the love for people in your very own heart.

Return to the weekly worship center order and continue. The scripture reading is Exodus 40:1–9.

MATERIALS

1. Desert box
2. Model of Tabernacle: buy one or build your own*
3. *Priest
4. Small basket for priest (3-inch)
5. Tabernacle artifacts: Ark, Altar of Incense, Table of Shewbread with 12 loaves of unleavened bread, Menorah, Holy Place (rectangular structure with veil to separate Holy of Holies), Laver, Altar of Burnt Offering, four cloth tentlike coverings (linen embroidered with red, blue, and purple; gray/black tweed for goat's hair; red fur for red-dyed rams' skins; long-haired fur for badgers' skins), linen fence
6. Small box or basket for Tabernacle artifacts (6-inch)
7. Tray for materials

---

*Sources:
Tabernacle Model to Make #2119 or *Build-a Tabernacle #2110* from Standard Publishing Company (8121 Hamilton Avenue, Cincinnati, Ohio 45231). These are cardboard. Paste on posterboard and laminate. Fill the boxes with solid material.
The Tabernacle of God in the Wilderness of Sinai by Paul F. Kiene (Grand Rapids: Zondervan Publishing House, 1977). This book explains how to build your own model.

CHILDREN

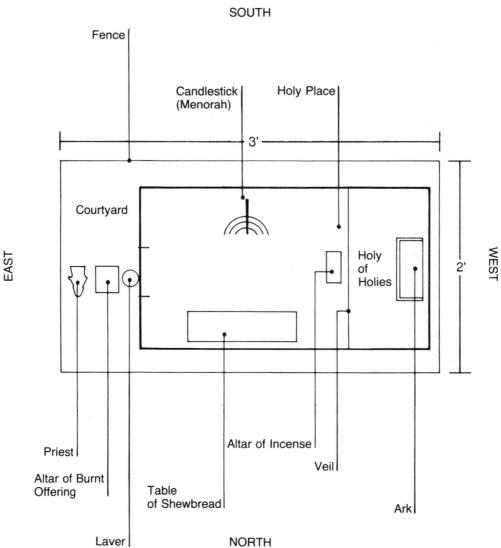

13

The Promised Land
Joshua 1–4

Walk slowly to the desert box and move it to the circle. Return to the sacred story shelf to get the tray with the **Promised Land** *materials. Carry it carefully with both hands to the circle and place it beside you. Sit quietly while you feel the story forming in you. Then say:*

This is the desert box.

Trace the edge of the desert box.

Inside is a small piece of the desert. . . . So many important things happen in the desert that we just have to have a small piece of it in our room.

Slowly move your hands over the sand, smoothing and molding it as the sand is transformed into the desert.

The desert is a strange and wild place. At night it is very cold, but in the day it is burning hot. There is almost no water at all. . . . The desert is always changing. The wind comes. And as it blows it shapes and molds. So the desert is never the same.

Mold the area where the Jordan will be and form some mounds in the bottom left of the box. Pause, place your hands in your lap, and sit back a moment. Then begin placing the people of God, including Joshua, in the desert box near the left-hand corner away from you as you say:

The people of God were still in the desert. They could have been living in the beautiful Promised Land with lots of food and water.

Smooth your hand over the Promised Land, the triangle of land to your right.

But they were afraid. "We cannot go into the Promised Land," they said. "The people are giants. We are like little grasshoppers. They will kill us." So they had to wander in the desert.

Move them slowly toward the middle of the box.

After many years they came to the Jordan River.

Press twelve black stones in the middle of the desert box and then place the dark blue felt for the Jordan River over them, running diagonally from the top at your left to the bottom right.

From there they could see the Promised Land.

Move some of the people up a mound to look over.

They could see Gilgal and the huge city of Jericho.

Trace Gilgal with your fingers. Then place the model of Jericho in the Promised Land. Move Joshua down toward the Jordan and let him stand looking across.

One day God said to Joshua:

Touch Joshua.

"Joshua. Don't be afraid. Lead the people of God into the Promised Land. Be strong. Have courage. I will be with you wherever you go."

Silently move Joshua along the Jordan, as though thinking. Then move him back to the people.

So Joshua said to the people, "Get ready. God will show us the way through the Jordan into the Promised Land. Don't be afraid."

Move Joshua toward four priests with the Ark.

The Ark of God led the way.

Move the Ark and the four priests to the Jordan. As they touch the Jordan, roll up one side and then the other and move them into the middle. Then move some of the people through.

God rolled back the Jordan . . . and they passed through on dry land.

Would you like to go through? When it is your turn you may come and choose one of the people of God to take through.

Name the children one at a time to take a figure through the Jordan.

When all were through, God said, "Take twelve stones from the middle of the Jordan."

Take the twelve stones out of the Jordan where the priests are standing and place them in a circle in the middle of the people. You may need to move the people around the stones.

Then Joshua said, "When your children ask 'What do these stones mean?' . . .

Move your hand in a circle, touching each stone slightly.

. . . you will say, 'The people of God passed through the Jordan on dry land into the Promised Land. For God dried up the Jordan just as God did the Red Sea, so that everyone may know God's power.' "

Move the priests out of the Jordan and roll the felt back.

When the kings of the land heard what God had done, they were afraid. And the people of God began to live in the Promised Land.

Responding to God's Word: Wondering Together

I wonder how the people felt when Joshua told them to get ready to go into the Promised Land? . . .

I wonder how it felt when God led them through the water into the Promised Land? . . .

I wonder what the people of God will do, now that they are in the Promised Land? . . .

Return to the weekly worship center order and continue. The scripture reading is Joshua 4:19–24 or Joshua 3:14–17.

MATERIALS

1. Desert box
2. Two pieces of dark blue felt, each 24 inches by 6 inches
3. *People of God, one for each child plus six extra, four priests to carry the Ark, and Joshua
4. Model of city of Jericho
5. Twelve black oval stones
6. Three baskets, for priests and Ark (6-inch), people (5-inch), and stones (5-inch)
7. Tray for materials

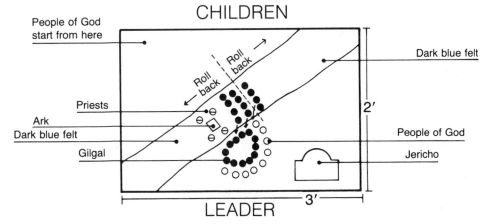

14

The Temple, a House for God
2 Samuel 5:1–7:17; 1 Kings 5–8;
2 Chronicles 6:1–11

*Walk slowly to the desert box and move it to the circle. Return to the sacred story shelf to get the trays with the **Temple and Ark** materials. Carry them carefully with two hands to the circle and place them beside you. Sit quietly while you feel the story forming in you. Then say:*

This is the desert box.

Trace the edge of the desert box.

Inside is a small piece of the desert. . . . So many important things happen in the desert that we just have to have a small piece of it in our room.

Slowly move your hands over the sand, smoothing and molding it as the sand is transformed into the desert.

The desert is a strange and wild place. . . . At night it is very cold, but in the day it is burning hot. There is almost no water at all. . . . The desert is always changing. The wind comes. And as it blows it shapes and molds. So the desert is never the same.

Pause, place your hands in your lap, and sit back a moment.

God loves us so much that God gave us the Ten Best Ways to Live. The people of God loved them so much, they made the Ark . . .

Present the Ark and place it in the sand on your right.

. . . to carry them with them on the way to the Promised Land. They even made a tent for God, called the Tabernacle, to keep the Ark in.

With your finger, outline a rectangular area for the Tabernacle in the sand and arch your hands over the Ark like a tent.

At last God led them through the waters of the Jordan River into the Promised Land. And they were home. But the people who lived there didn't want them. They fought with the people of God and tried to throw them out. And they even captured the Ark.

Remove the Ark.

After a long, long time, one of the people of God, King David, captured the city of Jerusalem.

Draw a ring in the sand of the desert box for Jerusalem. Leave a space for a gate.

King David built a palace, a beautiful house for himself. He didn't have to live in a tent in the desert anymore. Then King David found the Ark . . .

Put the Ark back in the sand and begin building the Tabernacle.

. . . and he brought it to Jerusalem and placed it in the tent for God. Then King David said, "I live in a beautiful house, but the Ark of God is in a tent. I will build a house for God." But God said, "No. Your son will build the house of God." So when Solomon, David's son, became king, he built a house for God. It was called the Temple.

Place the Temple next to the Tabernacle.

It took many people and many beautiful things to make the Temple. It had all the things that were in the tent for God.

Move each item, without explanation, into the Temple, leaving the Ark to last.

And in the Holy of Holies they put the Ark.

Sit back and pause.

If you go to Jerusalem today, you cannot find the Temple . . .

Trace the Temple and then touch the Ark.

. . . or the Ark. But that's all right. They are everywhere that people know God and love the Ten Best Ways to Live. That is what makes a holy place today. You can make such a place right where you are, right now.

Responding to God's Word: Wondering Together

I wonder how it felt to finally live in the land that God promised and to build a house for God? . . .

I wonder what it was like to build the Temple? . . .

I wonder who got to help build the Temple and how they did it? . . .

I wonder what it felt like to go to the Temple in Jerusalem? . . .

I wonder what the people did there and what they remembered when they went to the Temple? . . .

Now that the Temple and the Ark are gone, I wonder what the people of God do to be close to God? . . .

Return to the weekly worship center order and continue. The scripture reading is 2 Chronicles 6:1–11.

MATERIALS

1. Desert box
2. Tabernacle set with furnishings
3. Temple made from foam board, cardboard, or wood, slightly larger than the Tabernacle

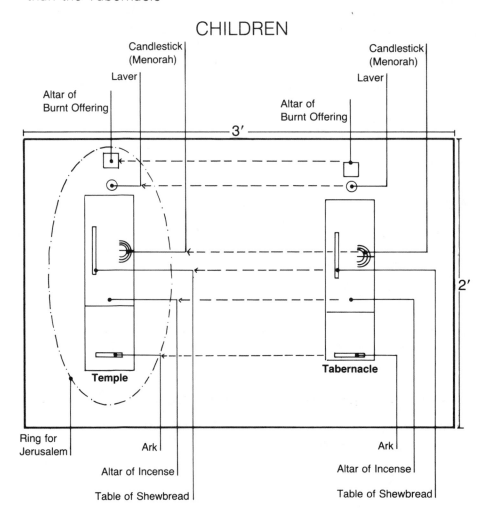

CHILDREN

LEADER

15

Exile and Return
Ezra 1–6

Walk slowly to the desert box and move it to the circle. Return to the sacred story shelf to get the tray with the **Exile** *materials. Carry it carefully with two hands to the circle and place it beside you. Sit quietly while you feel the story forming in you. Then say:*

This is the desert box.

Trace the edge of the desert box.

Inside is a small piece of the desert. . . . So many important things happen in the desert that we just have to have a small piece of it in our room.

Slowly move your hands over the sand, smoothing and molding it as the sand is transformed into the desert.

The desert is a strange and wild place. . . . At night it is very cold, but in the day it is burning hot. There is almost no water at all. . . . The desert is always changing. The wind comes. And as it blows it shapes and molds. So the desert is never the same.

Pause, place your hands in your lap, and sit back a moment. Draw a four-inch square in the sand. Put the people of God in the square as you say:

This is the city of Jerusalem, the Holy City of God. The people of God had lived in Jerusalem for a long time. . . . One day the king from another land came to Jerusalem. He wanted the Holy City for himself. So he and his army took it from the people of God. They burned the Temple, the house of God, and they tore down the walls around Jerusalem.

Smudge the outline of the square.

And the people of God were taken to a strange land . . .

Move the people from the city across the desert.

. . . the land of Babylon. They could not go home.

Place a heavy chain across the middle of the box.

They were in exile. Then a new king came to Babylon and took it for himself. This king began to let the people of God go back home. The first group went home to Jerusalem with Ezra. They built the Temple again.

Bring the first group to one end of the chain and move it enough for them to pass through. Then close it again.

Then the king let some more go home with Nehemiah. They built the wall around Jerusalem again.

Move the second group past the chain. Trace the square in the sand again and make it more distinct.

Some of the people decided to stay in Babylon, because for them it was no longer so strange.

Three of the people remain.

But most came home. It was good to be home, so they sang and danced.

Put the people in Jerusalem in a circle.

Responding to God's Word: Wondering Together

I wonder what it was like to see the Temple burning and the walls of Jerusalem being torn down? . . .

I wonder how it felt to be forced to go to a strange land, to live in exile? . . .

I wonder what it was like to live in Babylon? . . .

I wonder if God was with them in Babylon? . . .

Now that their old life is gone, I wonder what they will do? . . .

I wonder if God will show them a new way to live? . . .

I wonder what a new way would be like? . . .

I wonder if they lived the new way when they returned to Jerusalem to rebuild the Temple and the wall around Jerusalem? . . .

Return to the weekly worship center order and continue. The scripture reading is Ezra 1:2–4.

MATERIALS

1. Desert box
2. *People of God
3. Heavy chain, 2 feet long, to stretch across the desert box
4. Basket for people (4-inch)
5. Tray for materials

CHILDREN

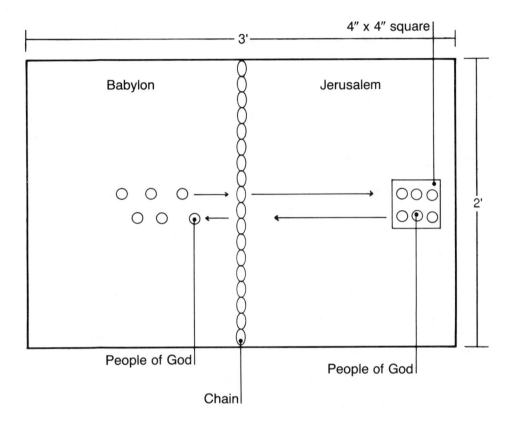

LEADER

16

How the Church Tells Time
Leviticus 23:1–3

Walk slowly to the rug box and get a rug. Carry it back over your shoulder, hugging it. Unroll it and smooth it out. Sit a moment, smile, and catch the eyes of all the children. Turn around and take the **Church Time Box** *from the shelf behind you. Slip the gold string inside the box into your fist, leaving about one and a half inches exposed between two fingers. Place the box on the far left of the rug.*

Sometimes it's very hard to tell what time it is. There are all kinds of time. I wonder how the church tells time? . . . Some say time is a line.

Lift your fist and begin slowly pulling out the gold string as you say:

It has a beginning . . . a middle . . . and an end.

Lay the whole string out on the rug and look at it. Point to the end at the right, the part taken hold of in the beginning, and say:

This could be the beginning and this the end.

Point to the other end.

Or this could be the beginning . . .

Continue pointing to one end and then to the other.

. . . and this could be the end. It's hard to tell beginnings and endings when time is in a line. . . . I know. Let's take the beginning that could be an ending and the ending that could be a beginning and tie them together.

Tie them together and place the circle on the floor. Touch the connecting point and say:

Now the ending is the beginning and the beginning is the ending. This is how the church tells time.

Lift the lid off the box and place the gold string around the puzzle, with the connecting point at the beginning of Advent.

This is the Church Year puzzle. It can show us how the church tells time. First we find the three special days. Here is Easter.

Pick out the Easter block and place it on the rug.

Here is Christmas.

Place Christmas to the right of Easter.

And here is (Ouch, it's hot, like fire!) Pentecost.

Place Pentecost to the left of Easter.

These are all the purple Sundays.

Group all the purple blocks on the rug.

These are all the white Sundays.

Group all the white blocks on the rug.

These are all the green Sundays.

Group all the green blocks on the rug.

Now let's see if we can make the puzzle of the church year. Let's begin with Christmas. It goes about here.

Present the Christmas block with the star on it and place it on the guideline of the puzzle board. Slide it about. You don't know exactly where it goes yet. Do the same with the others as you say:

And Easter goes about here. . . . And Pentecost goes about here.

Touch Christmas, as you say:

Christmas is the special day we celebrate the birth of Jesus and the mystery of how God became a person. Christmas is so special it takes four Sundays to get ready. We call this time Advent. The color for getting ready is purple. So we need four purple Sundays. But where do we put them?

Advent tells the beginning of the new church year and the ending of the old one. So let's put four purple Sundays right here . . . at the beginning that's an ending and the ending that's a beginning.

Count as you place the Advent Sundays in front of Christmas, with the first one touching the guide on the puzzle that marks the beginning of Advent (where the knot in the gold string is). Touch Easter, as you say:

Easter is the time we celebrate the mystery that Jesus died but is still with us. Easter is so special it takes six Sundays to get ready. Purple is the color for getting ready. So let's put six purple Sundays before Easter.

Count while you place six Sundays before Easter.

We are so happy that Jesus is alive, we celebrate Easter for six more Sundays. The color of Easter is white.

Touch Easter.

So let's put in six more Sundays of Easter.

Count as you put them in after Easter.

They go to Pentecost . . .

Touch Pentecost. Move it to touch the last Sunday of Easter if necessary.

. . . the day God gave the Holy Spirit so the church could say and do the amazing things that Jesus did.

Now we have the green Sundays left. They connect the Christmas time and the Easter time. The most we can have here is nine.

Count as you place nine between Christmas and Lent.

All the rest go after Pentecost.

Place the rest of the green blocks between Pentecost and Advent, but don't count them.

These words help us with the names of church time.

Touch the piece with Advent *written on it and move around the circle with your finger.*

This is Advent . . .

Hold up the piece with Advent *written on it for a moment, return it, and run your finger over the four Sundays of Advent.*

. . . the time the church gets ready to celebrate Christmas.

Continue picking up each piece named, returning it, and running your finger over the Sundays.

This is Epiphany, the time the church celebrates how God is known to the whole world. . . . This is Lent, the time the church gets ready to celebrate the mystery of Easter. . . . This is Easter, the time the church celebrates the mystery that Jesus died but is still with us. . . . This is Pentecost, the time the church celebrates God's gift of the Holy Spirit to the church.

Touch the markers for Christmas, Easter, and Pentecost, as you say:

These markers point to the three great days: Christmas, Easter, and Pentecost.

Look.

Point to the Church Year circle on the wall.

We have a big circle of the church year on our wall. It helps us tell church time. Today is the last Sunday of the church year.

(Or whatever Sunday you're doing this.)

Look. The marker is on the last Sunday after Pentecost. The marker points to the time it is.

Return to the weekly worship center order and continue. The scripture reading is Leviticus 23:1–3.

MATERIALS

1. *Wooden puzzle of the church year
2. Gold elastic string long enough to go around the circle of the wooden puzzle
3. Rug to put puzzle on
4. Colored cubes for the Sundays of the church year, as follows:
   Advent: four purple cubes for Protestants (or four blue cubes for Roman Catholics and Anglicans)
   Christmas: one white cube with gold star
   Epiphany: nine green cubes
   Lent: six purple cubes
   Easter: seven white cubes (the one for Easter Day has a gold cross on it)
   Pentecost: one red cube for the day and twenty-four green ones

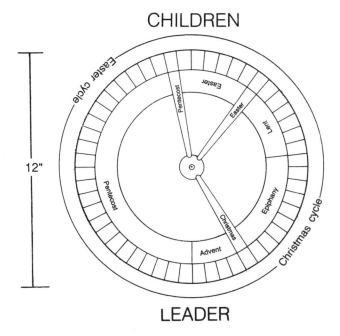

17

The Prophets
Show the Way to Bethlehem
(Advent I)
Isaiah 9:2; John 1:5

Go to the liturgical shelf and bring the materials for **Advent** *to the circle. Place the long white road in front of you. At the end of the road, to your left, place the square mat, purple side up. Put the model of Bethlehem on it. Then place the rolled purple underlay below the road to your far right, so that it will unroll to your left. Sit quietly while you feel the story forming in you. Then say:*

This is the season of Advent, the time we get ready to celebrate the mystery of Christmas, the time we are *all* on the way to Bethlehem.

Point toward Bethlehem.

But who will show us the way?

Run your hand over the road to Bethlehem. Then unroll the purple velvet underlay to expose the first space.

The prophets.

Present the first card and say:

Prophets listen to God. So they can show us the way.

Place the card on the underlay. Then present the figure of Isaiah and say:

Isaiah was a prophet who listened and spoke the word of God.

Place Isaiah on the road in front of the card.

He said one day the Messiah would be born. The Messiah would be like a light shining in darkness. This is what Isaiah said: "The people who walked in darkness have seen a great light; those who dwelt in a land of deep darkness, on them has light shined."

Place a purple candle between you and the card.

This is the candle of the prophets. It reminds us that prophets like Isaiah listen to God, so they can show us the way to Bethlehem.

Light the candle.

Let us enjoy the light of the prophets.

After an appropriate time for meditating, take the candle snuffer and say:

Now I will change the light.

Snuff the candle flame very slowly, catching the smoke in the snuffer cup and then releasing it. Watch the smoke wind upward into the room and disappear.

Before, the light was just here in one place. Now the light is in many places at once. The prophets can be with us always, in many ways and many places, all through the year. And who knows? Perhaps there is even a prophet here right now.

Look around the circle and look each child in the eyes. Wait a moment before putting the material away.

Responding to God's Word: Wondering Together

I wonder how the prophets listened to God? . . .

I wonder how they knew it was God who spoke? . . .

I wonder if there are still prophets today who can show us the way to Bethlehem? . . .

I wonder what the way to Bethlehem is like? . . .

Return to the weekly worship center order and continue. The scripture readings are Isaiah 9:2 and John 1:5.

MATERIALS FOR ADVENT, SESSIONS 17–20

1. *City of Bethlehem (cut skyscape from wood or white foam board)
2. Heavy mat board (16 by 20 inches), purple on one side and white on the other, to put under the city
3. Heavy white mat board for road (45 inches long by 8 inches wide)
4. Four heavy purple candles with wide bases (or three purple and one rose)
5. One white candle, taller and wider than the purple ones
6. *Set of Advent cards, four purple and one white, each 8 by 9 inches, made of poster board and laminated
7. Piece of purple velvet for underlay, 12 by 45 inches
8. Piece of white velvet, 12 by 12 inches, sewed to the purple underlay, to lay under the last (white) card
9. Purple cotton or lining fabric for backing, 12 by 45 inches
10. White brocade, 1 inch wide, 1 2/3 yards long, to separate the spaces for the cards on the underlay

11. Two sturdy baskets, 9 by 13 inches, for underlay and cards and for candles
12. Wooden crèche set*
13. *Wooden prophet figure
14. Safety matches in covered glass container
15. Candle snuffer

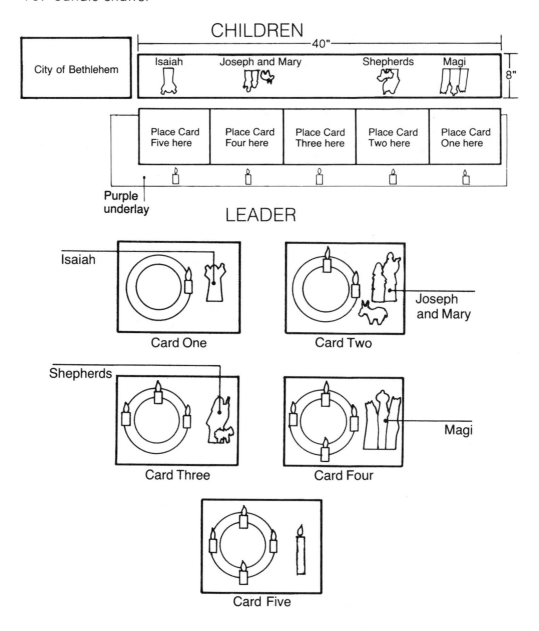

---

*Carved crèche set figures from Bethlehem may be ordered directly from the Division of Church World Service of the National Council of Churches or through The Bridge, Western Theological Seminary, Holland, MI 49423.

18

Mary and Joseph
Show the Way to Bethlehem
(Advent II)
Matthew 1–2; Luke 1–2

*Go to the liturgical shelf and bring the materials for **Advent** to the circle. Place the long white road in front of you. At the end of the road, to your left, place the square mat, purple side up. Put the model of Bethlehem on it. Then place the rolled purple underlay below the road to your far right, so that it will unroll to your left. Sit quietly while you feel the story forming in you. Then say:*

This is the season of Advent, the time we get ready to celebrate the mystery of Christmas, the time we are *all* on the way to Bethlehem.

Point toward Bethlehem.

But who will show us the way?

Run your hand over the road to Bethlehem. Then unroll the purple velvet underlay to expose the first space.

The prophets.

Present the first card and say:

Prophets listen to God. So they can show us the way.

Place the card on the underlay. Then present the figure of Isaiah and say:

Isaiah was a prophet who listened and spoke the word of God.

Place Isaiah on the road in front of the card.

He said one day the Messiah would be born. The Messiah would be like a light shining in darkness. This is what Isaiah said: "The people who walked in darkness have seen a great light; those who dwelt in a land of deep darkness, on them has light shined."

Place a purple candle between you and the card.

This is the candle of the prophets. It reminds us that prophets like Isaiah listen to God, so they can show us the way to Bethlehem.

Light the candle.

Let us enjoy the light of the prophets.

After an appropriate time for meditating, move Isaiah ahead two sections. Unroll the second section of the underlay. Present the second card and say:

Mary and Joseph are on the way to Bethlehem. They can show us the way. They have a secret. An angel came to them and said, "Do not be afraid. Be joyful. You will have God's special Son. You will name him Jesus."

Place the card on the underlay. Then turn to the Nativity set on the shelf behind you and take Mary and say:

Here is Mary . . .

Place Mary on the road in front of the card. Then present and place Joseph.

. . . and Joseph . . .

Present and place the donkey.

. . . and the donkey, who are on the way to Bethlehem, where Jesus will be born.

Take the purple candle and place it between you and the second card as you say:

This is the candle of the Holy Family. It reminds us not to be afraid, but to be joyful on the way to Bethlehem.

Light the candle.

Let us enjoy the light of the Holy Family.

After an appropriate time for meditating, take the candle snuffer and say:

Now I will change the lights.

Snuff the first candle flame very slowly, catching the smoke in the snuffer cup and then releasing it. Watch the smoke wind upward into the room and disappear as you say:

The light of the prophets . . . and the light of the Holy Family . . .

Snuff the other candle.

. . . can be with us always, in many ways and many places, all through the year.

Responding to God's Word: Wondering Together

I wonder how Mary felt when an angel spoke to her? . . .

I wonder how Joseph felt? . . .

I wonder what it would be like to have God's special child, Jesus? . . .

I wonder how they felt on the way to Bethlehem? . . .

Return to the weekly worship center order and continue. The scripture reading is Luke 1:26–33, 46–47.

19

The Shepherds
Show the Way to Bethlehem
(Advent III)
Matthew 1–2; Luke 1–2

Go to the liturgical shelf and bring the materials for **Advent** *to the circle. Place the long white road in front of you. At the end of the road, to your left, place the square mat, purple side up. Put the model of Bethlehem on it. Then place the rolled purple underlay below the road to your far right, so that it will unroll to your left. Sit quietly while you feel the story forming in you. Then say:*

This is the season of Advent, the time we get ready to celebrate the mystery of Christmas, the time we are *all* on the way to Bethlehem.

Point toward Bethlehem.

But who will show us the way?

Run your hand over the road to Bethlehem. Then unroll the purple velvet underlay to expose the first space.

The prophets.

Present the first card and say:

Prophets listen to God. So they can show us the way.

Place the card on the underlay. Then present the figure of Isaiah and say:

Isaiah was a prophet who listened and spoke the word of God.

Place Isaiah on the road in front of the card.

He said one day the Messiah would be born. The Messiah would be like a light shining in darkness. This is what Isaiah said: "The people who walked in darkness have seen a great light; those who dwelt in a land of deep darkness, on them has light shined."

Place a purple candle between you and the card.

This is the candle of the prophets. It reminds us that prophets like Isaiah listen to God, so they can show us the way to Bethlehem.

Light the candle.

Let us enjoy the light of the prophets.

After an appropriate time for meditating, move Isaiah ahead two sections. Unroll the second section of the underlay. Present the second card and say:

Mary and Joseph are on the way to Bethlehem. They can show us the way. They have a secret. An angel came to them and said, "Do not be afraid. Be joyful. You will have God's special Son. You will name him Jesus."

Place the card on the underlay. Then turn to the Nativity set on the shelf behind you and take Mary and say:

Here is Mary . . .

Place Mary on the road in front of the card. Then present and place Joseph.

. . . and Joseph . . .

Present and place the donkey.

. . . and the donkey, who are on the way to Bethlehem, where Jesus will be born.

Take a second purple candle and place it between you and the second card as you say:

This is the candle of the Holy Family. It reminds us not to be afraid, but to be joyful on the way to Bethlehem.

Light the candle.

Let us enjoy the light of the Holy Family.

After an appropriate time for meditating, move Isaiah ahead another two sections, and then the Holy Family, so the third section is clear. Unroll the third section of the underlay. Present the third card and say:

The shepherds are on the way to Bethlehem. They can show us the way. They have good news too. An angel came to them and said, "Do not be afraid. Be joyful. Today a Savior, God's special Son, is born in Bethlehem. You will find him lying in a manger."

Turn to the Nativity set on the shelf behind you and get the shepherds and sheep, one at a time, and place them on the road in front of the third card as you say:

Here are the shepherds . . . and their sheep . . . who are on the way to Bethlehem to see the special child who was born.

Place a purple candle (or a rose candle, if this is your church's practice) between you and the third card and say:

This is the candle of the shepherds. It reminds us of the good news: a Savior, the special Son of God, is born.

Light the candle.

Let us enjoy the light of the shepherds.

After an appropriate time for meditating, take the candle snuffer and say:

Now I will change the lights.

Snuff the first candle flame very slowly, catching the smoke in the snuffer cup and then releasing it. Watch the smoke wind upward into the room and disappear as you say:

The light of the prophets . . .

Snuff the second candle.

. . . and the light of the Holy Family . . .

Snuff the third candle.

. . . and the light of the shepherds . . . can be with us always, in many ways and many places, all through the year.

Responding to God's Word: Wondering Together

I wonder how the shepherds felt when an angel spoke to them? . . .

I wonder how they felt on the way to Bethlehem? . . .

I wonder if they will find the Savior, God's special child named Jesus? . . .

I wonder what will happen when they find Jesus? . . .

Return to the weekly worship center order and continue. The scripture reading is Luke 2:8–20.

20

The Magi
Show the Way to Bethlehem
(Advent IV)
Matthew 1–2; Luke 1–2

Go to the liturgical shelf and bring the materials for **Advent** *to the circle. Place the long white road in front of you. At the end of the road, to your left, place the square mat, purple side up. Put the model of Bethlehem on it. Then place the rolled purple underlay below the road to your far right, so that it will unroll to your left. Sit quietly while you feel the story forming in you. Then say:*

This is the season of Advent, the time we get ready to celebrate the mystery of Christmas, the time we are *all* on the way to Bethlehem.

Point toward Bethlehem.

But who will show us the way?

Run your hand over the road to Bethlehem. Then unroll the purple velvet underlay to expose the first space.

The prophets.

Present the first card and say:

Prophets listen to God. So they can show us the way.

Place the card on the underlay. Then present the figure of Isaiah and say:

Isaiah was a prophet who listened and spoke the word of God.

Place Isaiah on the road in front of the card.

He said one day the Messiah would be born. The Messiah would be like a light shining in darkness. This is what Isaiah said: "The people who walked in darkness have seen a great light; those who dwelt in a land of deep darkness, on them has light shined."

Place a purple candle between you and the card.

This is the candle of the prophets. It reminds us that prophets like Isaiah listen to God, so they can show us the way to Bethlehem.

Light the candle.

Let us enjoy the light of the prophets.

After an appropriate time for meditating, move Isaiah ahead two sections. Unroll the second section of the underlay. Present the second card and say:

Mary and Joseph are on the way to Bethlehem. They can show us the way. They have a secret. An angel came to them and said, "Do not be afraid. Be joyful. You will have God's special Son. You will name him Jesus."

Place the card on the underlay. Then turn to the Nativity set on the shelf behind you and take Mary and say:

Here is Mary . . .

Place Mary on the road in front of the card. Then present and place Joseph.

. . . and Joseph . . .

Present and place the donkey.

. . . and the donkey, who are on the way to Bethlehem, where Jesus will be born.

Take a second purple candle and place it between you and the second card as you say:

This is the candle of the Holy Family. It reminds us not to be afraid, but to be joyful on the way to Bethlehem.

Light the candle.

Let us enjoy the light of the Holy Family.

After an appropriate time for meditating, move Isaiah ahead another two sections, and then the Holy Family, so the third section is clear. Unroll the third section of the underlay. Present the third card and say:

The shepherds are on the way to Bethlehem. They can show us the way. They have good news too. An angel came to them and said, "Do not be afraid. Be joyful. Today a Savior, God's special Son, is born in Bethlehem. You will find him lying in a manger."

Turn to the Nativity set on the shelf behind you and get the shepherds and sheep, one at a time, and place them on the road in front of the third card as you say:

Here are the shepherds . . . and their sheep . . . who are on the way to Bethlehem to see the special child who was born.

Place a purple candle (or a rose candle, if this is your church's practice) between you and the third card and say:

This is the candle of the shepherds. It reminds us of the good news: a Savior, the special Son of God, is born.

Light the candle.

Let us enjoy the light of the shepherds.

After an appropriate time for meditating, move Isaiah and the Holy Family to the Bethlehem square, and the shepherds to the end of the road. Then unroll the fourth section of the purple underlay. Present the fourth card and say:

The Magi are on the way to Bethlehem. They can show us the way. The Magi saw a special star in the sky, a star for a king. They followed the star to Bethlehem, bringing gifts for the newborn king: gifts of gold, frankincense, and myrrh.

Place the card on the underlay. Then turn and get the Magi and the camel, placing them on the road one at a time.

Here are the Magi . . . and their camel.

Place a purple candle between you and the card and say:

This is the candle of the Magi. It reminds us of gifts, of God's gift of Christ the newborn king.

Light the candle.

Let us enjoy the light of the Magi.

After an appropriate time for meditating, take the candle snuffer and say:

Now I will change the lights.

Snuff the first candle flame very slowly, catching the smoke in the snuffer cup and then releasing it. Watch the smoke wind upward into the room and disappear as you say:

The light of the prophets . . .

Snuff the second candle,

. . . and the light of the Holy Family . . .

Snuff the third candle.

. . . and the light of the shepherds . . .

Snuff the fourth candle.

. . . and the light of the Magi . . . can be with us always, in many ways and many places, all through the year.

Responding to God's Word: Wondering Together

I wonder how the Magi felt when they saw the special star for a king? . . .

I wonder how they knew the star was special and others just saw a star? . . .

I wonder if it was hard for them to find the special king? . . .

I wonder why the Magi brought gifts? . . .

I wonder what it's like to be a baby and a king? . . .

I wonder what kind of king God's special one will be, and if you would like to live under this special king's rule? . . .

Return to the weekly worship center order and continue. The scripture reading is Matthew 2:1–12.

21

Christmas—
Meeting the Christ Child
Matthew 1–2; Luke 1–2

Go to the liturgical shelf and bring the materials for **Advent** *to the circle. Place the long white road in front of you. At the end of the road, to your left, place the square mat, white side up. Put the model of Bethlehem and the star on it. Then place the rolled purple underlay below the road to your far right, so that it will unroll to your left. Sit quietly while you feel the story forming in you. Then say:*

This is the season of Advent, the time we get ready to celebrate the mystery of Christmas, the time we are *all* on the way to Bethlehem.

Point toward Bethlehem.

But who will show us the way?

Run your hand over the road to Bethlehem. Then unroll the purple velvet underlay to expose the first space.

The prophets.

Present the first card and say:

Prophets listen to God. So they can show us the way.

Place the card on the underlay. Then present the figure of Isaiah and say:

Isaiah was a prophet who listened and spoke the word of God.

Place Isaiah on the road in front of the card.

He said one day the Messiah would be born. The Messiah would be like a light shining in darkness. This is what Isaiah said: "The people who walked in darkness have seen a great light; those who dwelt in a land of deep darkness, on them has light shined."

Place a purple candle between you and the card.

This is the candle of the prophets. It reminds us that prophets like Isaiah listen to God, so they can show us the way to Bethlehem.

Light the candle.

Let us enjoy the light of the prophets.

After an appropriate time for meditating, move Isaiah ahead two sections. Unroll the second section of the underlay. Present the second card and say:

Mary and Joseph are on the way to Bethlehem. They can show us the way. They have a secret. An angel came to them and said, "Do not be afraid. Be joyful. You will have God's special Son. You will name him Jesus."

Place the card on the underlay. Then turn to the Nativity set on the shelf behind you and take Mary and say:

Here is Mary . . .

Place Mary on the road in front of the card. Then present and place Joseph.

. . . and Joseph . . .

Present and place the donkey.

. . . and the donkey, who are on the way to Bethlehem, where Jesus will be born.

Take a second purple candle and place it between you and the second card as you say:

This is the candle of the Holy Family. It reminds us not to be afraid, but to be joyful on the way to Bethlehem.

Light the candle.

Let us enjoy the light of the Holy Family.

After an appropriate time for meditating, move Isaiah ahead two sections, and then the Holy Family, so the third section is clear. Unroll the third section of the underlay. Present the third card and say:

The shepherds are on the way to Bethlehem. They can show us the way. They have good news too. An angel came to them and said, "Do not be afraid. Be joyful. Today a Savior, God's special Son, is born in Bethlehem. You will find him lying in a manger."

Turn to the Nativity set on the shelf behind you and get the shepherds and sheep, one at a time, and place them on the road in front of the third card as you say:

Here are the shepherds . . . and their sheep . . . who are on the way to Bethlehem to see the special child who was born.

Place a purple candle (or a rose candle, if this is your church's practice) between you and the third card and say:

This is the candle of the shepherds. It reminds us of the good news: a Savior, the special Son of God, is born.

Light the candle.

Let us enjoy the light of the shepherds.

After an appropriate time for meditating, move Isaiah and the Holy Family to the Bethlehem square, and the shepherds to the end of the road. Unroll the fourth section of the purple underlay. Present the fourth card and say:

The Magi are on the way to Bethlehem. They can show us the way. The Magi saw a special star in the sky, a star for a king. They followed the star to Bethlehem, bringing gifts for the newborn king: gifts of gold, frankincense, and myrrh.

Place the card on the underlay. Then turn and get the Magi and the camel, placing them on the road one at a time.

Here are the Magi . . . and their camel.

Place a purple candle between you and the card and say:

This is the candle of the Magi. It reminds us of gifts, of God's gift of Christ, the newborn king.

Light the candle.

Let us enjoy the light of the Magi.

After an appropriate time for meditating, move the figures one at a time until they form a circle around the door of Bethlehem. (You will place the figure at the opening later.) Unroll the white section of the scroll. Present the last card and say:

Today is Christmas, the day we celebrate the mystery of God becoming a person. Today we are all at Bethlehem to meet the Christ child, the special Son of God.

Turn to the shelf and pick up the baby in the manger and present it.

Here is the newborn Christ child, lying in a manger bed . . .

From behind the model of Bethlehem move the Christ child through the gate of Bethlehem and place the figure in front of the gate, surrounded by the others, and continue saying:

. . . Christ the Light, a Light for the whole world.

Turn around and take the Christ candle from the shelf, place it on the floor behind the white section of the underlay, and say:

This is the Christ candle. It reminds us that Christ is Light. The light shines in the darkness, and the darkness has not overcome it.

Light the Christ candle and say:

Let us enjoy the Light of Christ.

After an appropriate time for meditating, take the candle snuffer and say:

Now I will change the lights.

Snuff the first candle flame very slowly, catching the smoke in the snuffer cup and then releasing it. Watch the smoke wind upward into the room and disappear as you say:

The light of the prophets . . .

Snuff the second candle.

. . . and the light of the Holy Family . . .

Snuff the third candle.

. . . and the light of the shepherds . . .

Snuff the fourth candle.

. . . and the light of the Magi . . .

Snuff the Christ candle,

. . . and the Light of Christ can be with us always in many ways and many places all through the year. So we can keep Christmas all year around.

Responding to God's Word: Wondering Together

I wonder how it feels to be in Bethlehem? . . .

I wonder how many got to Bethlehem and if they saw the Christ child? . . .

I wonder how they feel about this newborn baby? . . .

I wonder how this little baby is a light to the whole world, a light no darkness can overcome? . . .

I wonder how all these people and animals feel about the baby? . . .

I wonder how Jesus feels about them? . . .

I wonder how God feels? . . .

Return to the weekly worship center order and continue. The scripture reading is Luke 2:1–7.

22

The Boy Jesus
in the Temple
Luke 2:41–52

Walk slowly to the sacred story shelf and pick up the tray with the **Jesus in the Temple** *materials. Carry it carefully with two hands to the circle and place it beside you. Sit quietly while you feel the story forming in you. Then roll out the underlay and the beige felt road and smooth them as you say:*

Once every year the people of God go up to Jerusalem . . .

Place the Temple near the end of the road to your left. Place the teachers there.

. . . to celebrate the feast of the Passover, to remember how God led them through the waters to freedom.

Present and place each person on the road as you say their names.

This year Mary . . . and Joseph . . . and Jesus . . . were so happy because Jesus was old enough to go to the Temple all by himself.

Touch the Temple. Then move the figures to the Temple: first Jesus, then Mary and Joseph together.

Jesus went to the Temple to talk with God . . .

Move Jesus between the teachers. Parents remain on the road.

. . . and to hear the great teachers tell the stories of God.

Touch the teachers.

Then he went to eat the feast of the Passover with family and friends.

Move the family back to an imaginary house to your right, with Joseph facing the road, Jesus the Temple, and Mary with her back to the Temple. Pause for eating time. Then move Jesus back to the Temple.

After Passover, everyone started home.

Move Mary and Joseph down the road.

When evening came, Mary and Joseph went to Jesus' friends to get Jesus. But no one had seen him. They began looking for him.

Turn Mary and Joseph back toward Jerusalem, looking for Jesus.

They looked everywhere.

Continue looking until they get to the Temple. Leave them on the road with space for Jesus to stand almost between them.

At last they found Jesus at the Temple.

Move Jesus almost between them.

Mary said, "Where have you been? We have looked everywhere for you. We were so worried."

Jesus was surprised. "Why did you look everywhere for me? Didn't you know I would be in my Father's house?"

Pause.

They didn't understand. But they went home together.

Move them toward home, first Mary and Jesus together with Joseph following, then Jesus ahead and Mary and Joseph together. Move them to the end of the road.

And the boy, Jesus, grew to be a man. He grew taller and stronger. He grew in wisdom and love, and he was loved by God and loved by people.

Responding to God's Word: Wondering Together

I wonder how Jesus felt when he was finally old enough to go to the Temple all by himself? . . .

I wonder how Mary and Joseph felt when they couldn't find Jesus? . . .

I wonder why Jesus was surprised when his parents didn't know where he was? . . .

Touch the Temple.

I wonder what Jesus really meant when he called this his Father's house? . . .

Return to the weekly worship center order and continue. The scripture reading is Luke 2:41–52.

MATERIALS

1. Underlay of medium brown felt, 24 by 45 inches
2. Strip of beige felt for road, 45 inches long by 6 inches wide
3. *Solid wood temple, with steps
4. *Two wooden figures for teachers
5. *Wooden figures for Jesus, Mary, and Joseph
6. Two 5-inch baskets for figures: one for teachers and one for Jesus, Mary, and Joseph
7. Tray for materials

CHILDREN

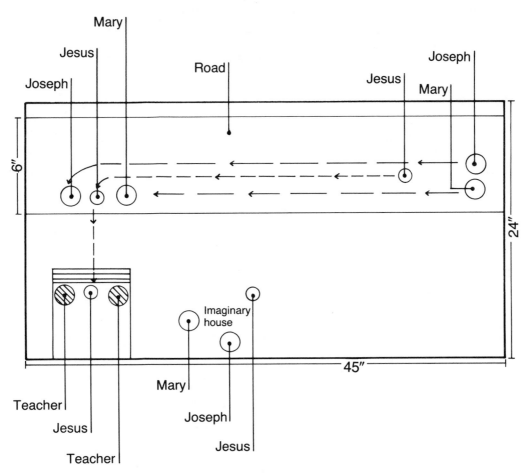

LEADER

23

Jesus Is Baptized
Matthew 3; Mark 1:1–11; Luke 3:1–22

Walk slowly to the desert box and move it to the circle. Return to the sacred story shelf to get the tray with the **Jesus' Baptism** *materials. Carry it carefully with two hands to the circle and place it beside you. Sit quietly while you feel the story forming in you. Then say:*

This is the desert box.

Trace the edge of the desert box.

Inside is a small piece of the desert. . . . So many important things happen in the desert that we just have to have a small piece of it in our room.

Slowly move your hands over the sand, smoothing and molding it as the sand is transformed into the desert.

The desert is a strange and wild place. At night it is very cold, but in the day it is burning hot. There is almost no water at all. . . . The desert is always changing. The wind comes. And as it blows it shapes and molds. So the desert is never the same.

Pause, place your hands in your lap, and sit back a moment. Then present John and place him in the desert box in front of you.

John the Baptist lived in the desert . . .

Pick up the blue felt river and unroll it diagonally across the desert box, starting at the left-hand corner near you. Smooth it out as you say:

. . . near the Jordan River. . . . The people of God came out to the desert to listen to John.

Present and move the people through the desert to John.

John said, "Get ready! God is sending someone special. The special Son of God is coming!" But they did not know how to get ready.

So John said, "Change the way you live. Do the Ten Best Ways to Live. And I will baptize you with water. You will be clean and new again." And John took the people through the water . . .

Have John take each person one at a time through the water and place them under the water in the pocket in the felt. Cup your hand over their heads.

... and baptized them. Then one day Jesus ...

Present Jesus and move him across the desert toward John.

... came to John and said, "Baptize me too." So they went through the water ...

Move them through the water and place Jesus under the water. Cup your hand over the head of Jesus.

... and John baptized Jesus.

Move them out of the water and say:

Then the heavens opened and the Spirit of God came to Jesus, ... and the voice of God said, "This is my Son."

Responding to God's Word: Wondering Together

I wonder how the people felt when John told them to change the way they live and get ready for the special Son of God? ...

I wonder if it was hard for them to change the way they lived? ...

I wonder how they felt when they went through the waters and went under the water to be baptized? ...

I wonder how they felt when they came out of the water? ...

I wonder if it was hard to wait for the special Son of God? ...

I wonder if they felt ready to be close to the special Son of God? ...

I wonder how you get ready to be close to the special Son of God? ...

Return to the weekly worship center order and continue. The scripture reading is Mark 1:9–11.

MATERIALS

1. Desert box
2. *Wooden figures of John the Baptist, three people, and Jesus
3. Two 5-inch baskets for figures: one for people and one for John and Jesus
4. Piece of dark blue felt 6 inches wide and 44 inches long (to fit diagonally across the desert box)
5. Second piece of dark blue felt, 6 inches wide and 22 inches long, to

be glued atop the half of the first piece that is nearer the children. Leave the end in the middle of the box open so figures can be slipped between the two pieces of felt for baptism.

6. Tray for materials

CHILDREN

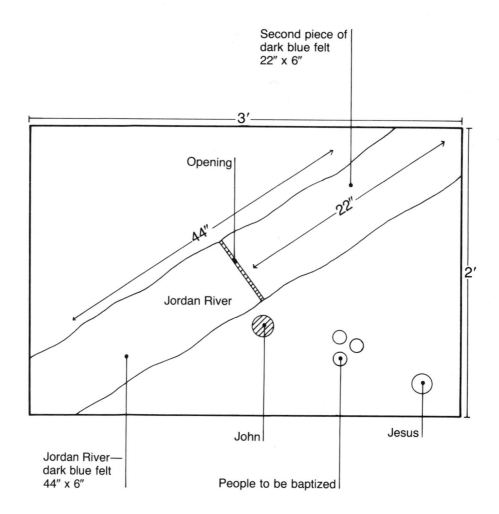

LEADER

24

Jesus in the Wilderness
Matthew 4:1–11; Mark 1:12–13; Luke 4:1–15

Walk slowly to the desert box and move it to the circle. Return to the sacred story shelf to get the tray with the **Wilderness** *materials. Carry it carefully with both hands to the circle. Sit quietly while you feel the story forming in you. Then say:*

This is the desert box.

Trace the edge of the desert box.

Inside is a small piece of the desert. . . . So many important things happen in the desert that we need a small piece of it in our center.

Slowly move your hands over the sand, smoothing and molding it as the sand is transformed into the desert.

The desert is a strange and wild place. At night it is very cold, but in the day it is burning hot. There is almost no water at all. . . . The desert is always changing.

Move sand as though wind is blowing and form a mound at the center of the edge of the box nearest you. The Temple will be placed here later.

The wind comes and as it blows it shapes and molds. So the desert is never the same.

Place the figure of Jesus at the center of the edge of the desert box closest to you, and move it ahead to the center of the box as you say:

Jesus was led by the Spirit of God into the desert. For forty days and forty nights, he stayed alone in the desert, . . . talking with God, . . . and wondering which way he should go.

Move Jesus through the desert toward your right to the front corner.

Jesus had been in the desert a very long time, and he had nothing to eat. He was very hungry.

Place some stones near Jesus.

Then the evil one came to Jesus and said, "If you really are the special Son of God, turn these stones into bread."

Jesus was very hungry. Bread would taste so good. Jesus wondered. . . . Then Jesus said, *"No!"*

Turn Jesus' back to the stones.

Jesus said, "The scripture says, 'We need more than bread to live. We must also do what God says.' "

Move Jesus slowly to the center.

Then the evil one came to Jesus a second time and took him to Jerusalem, the holy city of God.

Place the Temple in the middle of the edge of the sand near you.

Here the evil one set Jesus on the highest point of the Temple.

Move Jesus up to the highest point of the Temple.

The evil one said, "If you really are the special Son of God, prove it. Throw yourself down; for the scripture says, 'God will send angels to save you.' "

Jesus wondered. . . . If angels saved him everyone would know he was special and they would follow him. Then Jesus said, *"No!* The scripture says, 'You shall not tempt the Lord your God.' "

Move Jesus down from the Temple and back to the center. Then move him to the far corner toward your left.

Then the evil one came to Jesus a third time and took him to a very high mountain.

Place the mountain toward the edge of the desert on your left and move Jesus to the top of it.

"Look," said the evil one. "Here are all the nations of the world. Look how wonderful they are. I will give all of them to you, if you will worship me."

It would be wonderful to be king of all these nations. Jesus wondered. . . . Then Jesus said, *"No!* Go away, Satan! The scripture says, 'You shall worship God only.' "

Turn Jesus around and down the back of the mountain. Then move him to the center of the desert in front of the Temple.

The evil one left Jesus. And Jesus was filled with the Spirit of God. Jesus returned safely home.

Move Jesus to the edge of the desert box opposite you.

And in the power of the Holy Spirit, Jesus began to tell anyone who would listen about a special kingdom, the Kingdom of God.

Responding to God's Word: Wondering Together

I wonder what it was like to be alone in the desert for such a long time? . . .

I wonder what Jesus and God talked about in the desert? . . .

I wonder how Jesus felt when the evil one was near him? . . .

I wonder if it was hard to say *"No!"?* . . .

I wonder how Jesus felt when the Spirit of God filled him? . . .

I wonder what the people thought when they heard Jesus telling about the Kingdom of God? . . .

Return to the weekly worship center order and continue. The scripture reading is Matthew 4:1–11 or Mark 1:12–13.

MATERIALS

1. Desert box
2. *Wooden figure of Jesus
3. Three small stones
4. Basket for stones (4-inch)
5. Temple (from Session 22)
6. Large rock with flat top
7. Tray for materials

CHILDREN

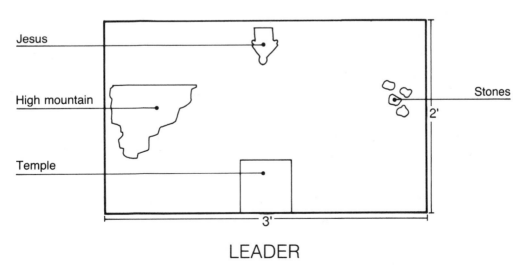

LEADER

25

The Mustard Seed
Matthew 13:31–32

Walk slowly to the parable shelf and pick up the **Mustard Seed** *box. Carry it to the circle. Put the box down in front of you and look at it. Sit quietly while you feel the parable forming in you. Then touch the box gently, with wonder, and say:*

I wonder if this is a parable? Hmm. It might be. Parables are very precious, like gold, and this box is gold.

Gently run your hand over the lid.

This looks like a present.

Lift the box and admire it like a present.

Well, parables are like presents. They have already been given to us. We can't buy them, or take them, or steal them. They are already ours. . . . There's another reason why this might be a parable. It has a lid.

Trace the lid of the box with your fingers.

And sometimes parables seem to have lids on them. But when you lift the lid of a parable there is something very precious inside. . . . I know. Let's take off the lid and see if this is a parable.

Lift the lid and peek inside. Put the lid back on and move the box to your side. Then open the lid just enough to take out the materials but not enough for the children to see inside. Take out the gold underlay with wonder and spread it out, as you say:

I wonder what this could be? . . . It is the color yellow. I wonder what could be so yellow? Hmm.

As the children respond, incorporate their responses into your story. Don't discuss them. For example:

It could be the sun . . . or a big yellow ball. . . .

Hide the rolled-up green felt mustard tree in your left hand. You will be taking the mustard seed out of the box to plant with your right hand (or vice versa). Sit back a moment and then say:

Once there was someone who said such amazing things, and did such wonderful things, that people began to follow him. As they followed, he told them about a kingdom: the Kingdom of Heaven. But they did not understand. They had never been to such a place. And they didn't know anyone who had. They didn't even know where it was. So one day they simply had to ask him, "What is the Kingdom of Heaven like?"

And he said, "The Kingdom of Heaven is like a grain of mustard seed . . .

Reach into the box and take out something so small it cannot be seen—actually nothing—since mustard seeds from Israel are too small to be seen unless one is very close.

. . . which a person took . . . and sowed in a field.

Press down the seed as if planting, with your hand hiding the rolled-up felt shrub.

It is the smallest of all the seeds, and it grew . . .

Slowly unroll the shrub.

. . . and it grew . . . and it grew.

When it has grown, the mustard is the greatest of shrubs and becomes a tree, so that the birds of the air come . . .

Take the container with the birds and place a few of the flying birds approaching the shrub.

. . . and make nests there . . .

Place a few of the nests on the branches.

. . . in its branches."

Place a few of the sitting birds in the nests.

Responding to God's Word: Wondering Together

In a container, have enough flying birds, nests, and birds sitting in nests so that each child can place one or more on the shrub. Pass the container around the circle. The children will come forward one at a time to place their objects on the shrub.

I wonder if you would like to put nests and birds in the tree too? . . .

I wonder if these birds have names? . . .

I wonder how the birds feel about this tree? . . .

I wonder where the birds were coming from? . . .

I wonder if the birds were happy to find such a tree? . . .

I wonder how many birds could really live in this tree? . . .

I wonder if this tree has a name? . . .

I wonder if this tree could be put back into the seed after it is grown? . . .

I wonder what this tree might really be? . . .

I wonder where this whole place might really be? . . .

Return to the weekly worship center order and continue. The scripture reading is Matthew 13:31–32.

MATERIALS

1. Gold box (business-size envelope box wrapped in plain gold foil paper)
2. Large yellow felt circle, seed-shaped (smaller at one end to accommodate the spreading of the branches at the other end), 33 to 34 inches in diameter at widest part
3. *Mustard tree cut from green felt, 29 to 30 inches tall when unrolled
4. *Birds, at least one per child, backed with poster board and laminated
5. *Nests, at least one per child, backed with poster board and laminated
6. Three small baskets for imaginary seed (3-inch), birds (4-inch), and nests (4-inch)

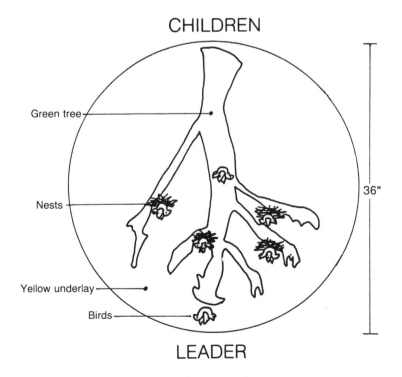

26

The Leaven
Matthew 13:33

Walk slowly to the parable shelf and pick up the **Leaven** *box. Carry it to the circle. Put the box down in front of you and look at it. Sit quietly while you feel the parable forming in you. Then touch the box gently, with wonder, and say:*

I wonder if this is a parable? Hmm. It might be. Parables are very precious, like gold, and this box is gold.

Gently run your hand over the lid.

This looks like a present.

Lift the box and admire it like a present.

Well, parables are like presents. They have already been given to us. We can't buy them, or take them, or steal them. They are already ours. . . . There's another reason why this might be a parable. It has a lid.

Trace the lid of the box with your fingers.

And sometimes parables seem to have lids on them. But when you lift the lid of a parable, there is something very precious inside. . . . I know. Let's take off the lid and see if this is a parable.

Lift the lid and peek inside. Put the lid back on and move the box to your side. Then open the lid just enough to take out the materials but not enough for the children to see inside. Take out the tan-colored underlay with wonder and spread it out, as you say:

I wonder what this could be? . . . It's a different color. It's not really yellow. And it's not really brown. I wonder what it could be?

Incorporate the responses of the children into the story. Don't discuss them.

It could be a mud puddle. . . .

Sit back a moment, then say:

Once there was someone who said such amazing things, and did such wonderful things, that people began to follow him. As they followed, he told them about a kingdom: the Kingdom of Heaven. But they did not understand. They had never been to such a place. And they didn't know anyone who had. They didn't even know where it was. So one day they simply had to ask him, "What is the Kingdom of Heaven like?"

And he said, "The Kingdom of Heaven is like leaven . . .

Take the leaven triangle from the box and place it on the lower part of the underlay near the center.

. . . which a person took . . .

Place the person and the table in the center of the underlay. Place the leaven in the person's hand.

. . . and hid . . .

Remove the three flour containers and the flask from the box and place them on the table.

. . . in three measures of flour.

Move the leaven to the flour and mix them together. Pour in the water and continue mixing.

And as this person waited, it grew . . .

Place the partly risen loaf over the dough.

. . . and it grew . . .

Place the half-risen loaf over the dough.

. . . and it grew . . .

Place the fully risen loaf over the dough.

. . . till it was all leavened."

Sit back and pause.

Responding to God's Word: Wondering Together

Touch the loaf.

I wonder if this loaf has a name? . . .

Motion with your hands around the bread.

I wonder if you could take the loaf of bread and put it back to where it was before the leaven was hidden in it? . . .

I wonder what the leaven might really be? . . .

Point to the person.

I wonder if this person has a name? . . .

I wonder what this person was doing while the loaf was being leavened? . . .

I wonder how this person felt while the loaf was being leavened? . . .

I wonder if this person spoke any words while the loaf was being leavened? . . .

I wonder why the person put the leaven in the loaf? . . .

Point to the table.

I wonder if you have ever been close to this table? . . .

I wonder where this whole place could really be? . . .

I wonder if you would like to make something that shows how this parable feels to you? . . .

> *Return to the weekly worship center order and continue. The scripture reading is Matthew 13:33.*

MATERIALS

1. Gold box
2. Triangular underlay of tan-colored felt with corners rounded, about 30 by 36 inches
3. *Figure of a woman, mounted on poster board and laminated.
4. *Three round white pieces (to represent the measure of flour) mounted on white poster board and laminated
5. *Tiny laminated yellow triangle (to represent the leaven)
6. *Flask, mounted on poster board and laminated
7. *Three pieces, forming a loaf of bread large enough to cover the measures of flour, made from poster board and laminated
8. Two 4-inch baskets for measures of flour and leaven and flask
9. *Table, colored, mounted on poster board, and laminated

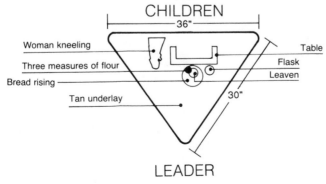

27

The Great Pearl
Matthew 13:45–46

*Walk slowly to the parable shelf and pick up the **Great Pearl** box. Carry it to the circle. Put the box down in front of you and look at it. Sit quietly while you feel the parable forming in you. Then touch the box gently, with wonder, and say:*

I wonder if this is a parable? Hmm. It might be. Parables are very precious, like gold, and this box is gold.

Gently run your hand over the lid.

This looks like a present.

Lift the box and admire it like a present.

Well, parables are like presents. They have already been given to us. We can't buy them, or take them, or steal them. They are already ours. . . . There's another reason why this might be a parable. It has a lid.

Trace the lid of the box with your fingers.

And sometimes parables seem to have lids on them. But when you lift the lid of a parable, there is something very precious inside. . . . I know. Let's take off the lid and see if this is a parable.

Lift the lid and peek inside. Put the lid back on and move the box to your side. Then open the lid just enough to take out the materials but not enough for the children to see inside. Take out the white underlay with wonder and spread it out, as you say:

I wonder what this could be? . . . This is so white. I wonder what could be so white? Hmm.

Incorporate the responses of the children into the story. Don't discuss them. For example:

It could be a cloud . . . or a snowball . . . or a beautiful table. . . . Let's see if there is more that can help us figure out if this could be a parable.

Take out a long brown "house."

There is this. There's an inside and an outside. And there are more.

Place the "houses" on the underlay.

This is different. But it's sort of the same. It could be a house.

Place all the merchant's goods in the house to your left, farthest from you. Place the table in the house in the center near you. Then put the seller behind the table. Now take the pearls out of the little box and place one in each house. The pearls go on the table in the two houses. When all the pieces are in place, sit back a moment and then say:

Once there was someone who said such amazing things, and did such wonderful things, that people began to follow him. As they followed, he told them about a kingdom: the Kingdom of Heaven. But they did not understand. They had never been to such a place. And they didn't know anyone who had. They didn't even know where it was. So one day they simply had to ask him, "What is the Kingdom of Heaven like?"

And he said, "The Kingdom of Heaven is like a merchant . . .

Take the merchant out of the box and place him beside the far left-hand house.

. . . who buys and sells fine pearls. He goes in search of the Great Pearl.

Have the merchant slowly travel to each house, pick up each pearl and inspect it, then put it back.

And when he finds it . . .

At the seller's house, have the merchant pick up the pearl with obvious respect and look at it.

. . . he goes and exchanges all that he has . . .

Return the merchant to his house to begin carrying everything to the seller, leaving the bed until last.

. . . he exchanges everything . . .

Roll up the house, and carry it to the seller. Have the merchant pick up the pearl and move to where his house was, as you say:

. . . for the Great Pearl."

Pause and sit back for a moment.

Responding to God's Word: Wondering Together

Point to the Pearl and then hold it up to inspect it again.

I wonder what could be so great that the merchant would exchange everything he had for the Great Pearl? . . .

I wonder how this pearl could be the Great Pearl, and all the other pearls could be just pearls? . . .

I wonder what the Great Pearl could really be? . . .

I wonder how this person could ever give away the Great Pearl? . . .

I wonder who has the most now, this person or this person? . . .

Point to the two persons.

I wonder if you know the merchant? . . .

I wonder if the merchant has a name? . . .

I wonder if the merchant is happy where he is? . . .

Touch the seller.

I wonder if you've ever been close to this person? . . .

Touch the table.

Or if you've ever been close to this table? . . .

Touch the seller.

I wonder if this person has a name? . . .

Trace the seller's house.

I wonder where this place could really be? . . .

Trace the outline of the whole underlay.

I wonder where this whole place could really be? . . .

Return to the weekly worship center order and continue. The scripture reading is Matthew 13:45–46.

MATERIALS

1. Gold box
2. Large white felt circle, 40 inches in diameter
3. Brown felt outlines for houses, 2 large, 3 smaller
4. Two money pouches, colored, mounted on poster board, and laminated
5. *Variety of possessions in merchant's house: rug, table, chair, water jar, oil jar, flour jar, lamp, money bags, pearl, and bed, colored, mounted on poster board, and laminated
6. Five pearls, all the same size
7. Beautiful white container for pearls (2½ inches)
8. *Figure of merchant, colored, mounted on poster board, and laminated

9. *Figure of the seller of pearls, colored, mounted on poster board, and laminated
10. *Table

CHILDREN

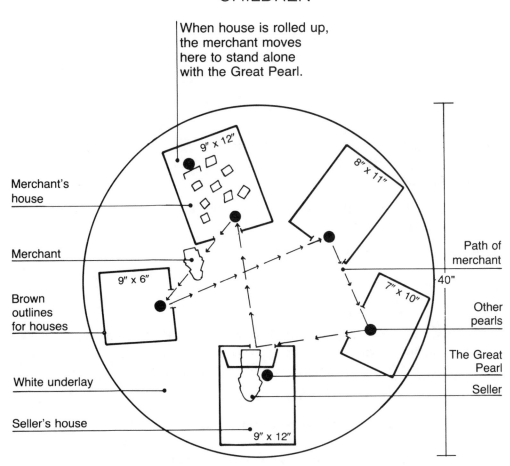

When house is rolled up, the merchant moves here to stand alone with the Great Pearl.

Merchant's house

9" x 12"

8" x 11"

Merchant

Path of merchant

Brown outlines for houses

9" x 6"

40"

7" x 10"

Other pearls

The Great Pearl

White underlay

Seller

Seller's house

9" x 12"

LEADER

28

The Sower
Matthew 13:3–8; Mark 4:3–8; Luke 8:5–8

*Walk slowly to the parable shelf and pick up the **Sower** box. Carry it to the circle. Put the box down in front of you and look at it. Sit quietly while you feel the parable forming in you. Then touch the box gently, with wonder, and say:*

I wonder if this is a parable? Hmm. It might be. Parables are very precious, like gold, and this box is gold.

Gently run your hand over the lid.

This looks like a present.

Lift the box and admire it like a present.

Well, parables are like presents. They have already been given to us. We can't buy them, or take them, or steal them. They are already ours. . . . There's another reason why this might be a parable. It has a lid.

Trace the lid of the box with your fingers.

And sometimes parables seem to have lids on them. But when you lift the lid of a parable, there is something very precious inside. . . . I know. Let's take off the lid and see if this is a parable.

Lift the lid and peek inside. Put the lid back on and move the box to your side. Then open the lid just enough to take out the materials but not enough for the children to see inside. Take out the rust-colored underlay with wonder and spread it out, as you say:

I wonder what this could be? . . .

Incorporate the responses of the children into your story. Do not discuss them.

It could be a road, or a field. . . .

Sit back a moment and then say:

Once there was someone who said such amazing things, and did such wonderful things, that people began to follow him. One day he told them this parable. A sower went out to sow.

Present and place the sower on the end of the felt to your right.

And as the sower went along sowing seeds . . .

Scatter some imaginary seeds with your hand.

. . . some fell on the path. The birds came and ate them.

Put the birds on the underlay at the end where the sower is and then move the sower to the next section.

Some of the seeds fell on the rocks.

Present and place the rocks on the underlay and scatter imaginary seeds with your hand.

The little seeds began to grow. But they could not put their roots down very far. The sun came and all the little plants died.

Move the sower on to the next section.

Some seeds fell among thorns.

Present and place the thorns on the underlay and scatter imaginary seeds.

When the little seeds put down their roots, the thorns choked them.

Move the sower to the next section.

Other seeds fell on the good soil . . .

Present and place the good soil on the underlay and scatter imaginary seeds.

. . . and when these little seeds put down their roots, they grew, and they grew, and they grew. At the harvest they brought forth grain . . .

Place the bags on the underlay.

. . . some thirty, some sixty, and some one hundred bushels.

Responding to God's Word: Wondering Together

Now I wonder how the seeds felt that fell on the path? . . .

I wonder how the birds felt? . . .

I wonder if the birds have names? . . .

I wonder what the seed felt about the birds? . . .

I wonder how the seeds felt that fell among the rocks? . . .

I wonder how the sun felt about the little seeds? . . .

I wonder how the seeds felt that fell in the thorns? . . .

I wonder what the thorns felt about the little seeds? . . .

I wonder how the seeds felt that fell in good soil? . . .

I wonder how the good soil felt about the little seeds? . . .

I wonder how so much grain could come from the little seeds? . . .

Return to the weekly worship center order and continue. The scripture reading is Matthew 13:3–8.

MATERIALS

1. Gold box
2. Strip of rust-brown felt, 57 inches long and 12 inches wide
3. *Figure sowing seeds, colored, mounted on poster board, and laminated
4. Birds, colored, mounted on poster board, and laminated (use pattern for session 25)
5. Small basket for birds (3-inch)
6. *Strip of rocks, colored, mounted on poster board, and laminated
7. *Strip of thorns, colored, mounted on poster board, and laminated
8. *Strip of furrowed earth, colored, mounted on poster board, and laminated
9. *Three sacks of grain of increasing size
10. Basket for three sacks (6-inch)

CHILDREN

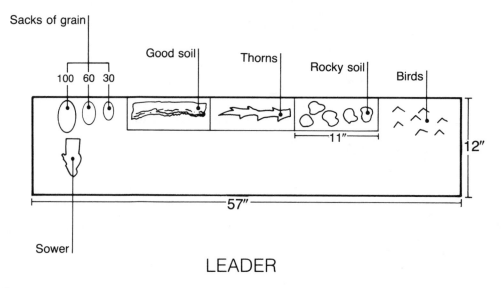

LEADER

29

The Good Samaritan
Luke 10:25–37

Walk slowly to the parable shelf and pick up the **Good Samaritan** *box. Carry it to the circle. Put the box down in front of you and look at it. Sit quietly while you feel the parable forming in you. Then touch the box gently, with wonder, and say:*

I wonder if this is a parable? Hmm. It might be. Parables are very precious, like gold, and this box is gold.

Gently run your hand over the lid.

This looks like a present.

Lift the box and admire it like a present.

Well, parables are like presents. They have already been given to us. We can't buy them, or take them, or steal them. They are already ours. . . . There's another reason why this might be a parable. It has a lid.

Trace the lid of the box with your fingers.

And sometimes parables seem to have lids on them. But when you lift the lid of a parable there is something very precious inside. . . . I know. Let's take off the lid and see if this is a parable.

Lift the lid and peek inside. Put the lid back on and move the box to your side. Then open the lid just enough to take out the materials but not enough for the children to see inside. Take out the burlap underlay with wonder and spread it out, as you say:

I wonder what this could be? . . . It is very rough. I wonder what could be so rough? . . . It's brown. I wonder what such a brown place could be?

Bring out the road.

I wonder what this could be? I could put one end here and the other end here.

Place one end near you and roll it out to the other end.

169

I wonder what it could be? . . . Let's see if there is something else that could help. There are these.

Place Jerusalem to the left at the end near you and Jericho at the other end of the road. Put the dark blue felt rocks beside the road on your right. Place the two robbers behind the rocks. Sit back a moment, then say:

Once there was someone who said such amazing things, and did such wonderful things, that people began to follow him. One day a lawyer asked him, "What is the most important law?" And he answered, "You already know."

The lawyer said, "Yes. We are to love God and love our neighbors. . . . But who is my neighbor?"

Place the traveler at Jerusalem.

So he told a parable. A person . . .

Begin moving him.

. . . was going down from Jerusalem to Jericho . . .

Point to the cities.

. . . and robbers . . .

Move the robbers out from behind the rocks and cross them over the traveler.

. . . came and attacked him . . . and hurt him . . . and took everything that he had . . . and left him by the road, half dead.

Remove the robbers and return them to the box and turn the traveler over by the side of the road.

A great priest from the Temple in Jerusalem was going down the road.

Move the priest slowly from Jerusalem.

When he saw him . . .

Stop the priest for a moment.

. . . he passed by on the other side.

Move the priest to the far side, past the injured traveler, and then return him to the center of the road and on to Jericho.

A Levite, a person who also worked at the Temple, was going down to Jericho.

Move the Levite slowly from Jerusalem.

When he saw him . . .

Stop him a moment.

. . . he passed by on the other side.

Use the same movement as with the priest.

But a Samaritan . . .

Begin moving the Samaritan.

. . . who was not even from the same country . . . came to where he was.

Pause.

And when he saw him, he had compassion . . .

Pause again.

. . . and went to him.

Move to the traveler.

He put medicine and bandages on his cuts and put him on his donkey . . .

Cover the traveler with the picture of the injured man and the donkey.

. . . and brought him to an inn . . .

Move on toward Jericho.

. . . and stayed with him all night. He told the innkeeper that the man could stay until he was well and he would pay for it all.

Pause. Sit back.

Now, which of these three . . .

Place the priest, the Levite, and the Samaritan with the robbers at the top of the underlay in a line facing the children.

. . . was a neighbor to the person who was hurt, and robbed, and left by the side of the road half dead?

Responding to God's Word: Wondering Together

I wonder if the person who was left by the side of the road half dead has a name? . . .

I wonder where the road was really going? . . .

I wonder who was a neighbor to the robber? . . .

I wonder who was a neighbor to the priest? . . .

I wonder who was a neighbor to the Levite? . . .

I wonder who was a neighbor to the Samaritan? . . .

I wonder how a Samaritan could be a neighbor? . . .

Return to the weekly worship center order and continue. The scripture reading is Luke 10:25–37.

MATERIALS

1. Gold box
2. Large dark brown piece of burlap, 36 by 36 inches
3. Beige strip of burlap for road, 48 inches long by 6 inches wide
4. Two dark blue irregular felt circles for rocks, 8 by 11 inches
5. *City of Jerusalem, mounted on poster board and laminated
6. *City of Jericho (made to look distant by being drawn on a smaller scale), mounted on poster board and laminated
7. *Six colored figures, mounted on poster board and laminated: two robbers, a traveler, a priest, a Levite, and a Samaritan
8. *Circular piece of poster board, laminated, showing the Samaritan putting the traveler on a donkey (large enough to put over the figures of Samaritan and traveler)

CHILDREN

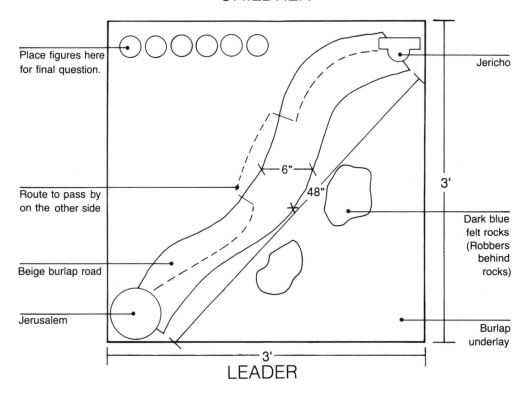

30

The Great Banquet
Luke 14:15–24

*Walk slowly to the parable shelf, and pick up the **Great Banquet** box. Carry it to the circle. Put it down in front of you and look at it. Sit quietly while you feel the parable forming in you. Then touch the box gently, with wonder, and say:*

I wonder if this is a parable? Hmm. It might be. Parables are very precious, like gold, and this box is gold.

Gently run your hand over the lid.

This looks like a present.

Lift the box and admire it like a present.

Well, parables are like presents. They have already been given to us. We can't buy them, or take them, or steal them. They are already ours. . . . There's another reason why this might be a parable. It has a lid.

Trace the lid of the box with your fingers.

And sometimes parables seem to have lids on them. But when you lift the lid of a parable there is something very precious inside. . . . I know. Let's take off the lid and see if this is a parable.

Lift the lid and peek inside. Put the lid back on and move the box to your side. Then open the lid just enough to take out the materials but not enough for the children to see inside. Take out the green felt underlay and smooth it out, as you say:

I wonder what this could be? It's so green. It's shaped like a square. It could be a blanket . . . or a rug. Let's see if there's more.

Take out the large table, present it, and place it in the center.

Hmm. This looks like a table.

Sit back a moment, then say:

173

Once there was someone who said such amazing things, and did such wonderful things, that people began to follow him. As they followed, he told them about a kingdom: the Kingdom of Heaven. But they did not understand. They had never been to such a place. And they didn't know anyone who had.

So one day he said, "The Kingdom of Heaven is like this: Once a person invited many people to a great feast.

Place person behind the table. Then fill the whole table with food.

When the feast was ready, the servant said to the guests, 'Come, for all is now ready.'

Motion across the table.

But they all made excuses. The first said, 'I just bought a field and I have to go and see it.

Take the field from the box and present it. Lay the field flat on your hand and circle the table as you say:

Please excuse me.'

Place field back in box.

Another said, 'I just bought five yoke of oxen and I have to go and try them out.

Take the oxen from the box and present them. Lay the oxen flat on your hand and circle the table as you say:

Please excuse me.'

Place the oxen back in the box.

Still another said, 'I just got married, so I cannot come.

Take the wedding rings out of the box and present them. Lay the rings flat on your hand and circle the table as you say:

Please excuse me.'

Pause. Touch the food on the table. Then say:

When the servant told his master, he said, 'Go quickly to the streets and alleys of the city and bring in the poor . . .

Take and present the poor persons from the box, and place at the table. Continue with the others as named.

. . . the crippled . . . the blind . . . and the lame.' But still there was room.

Point to the empty spaces and say:

'Go out to the highways and roads and get people to come, so my house will be filled.' "

Put others around the table. Then sit back.

Responding to God's Word: Wondering Together

I wonder how it felt to be invited to this great feast? . . .

I wonder if these people have names? . . .

I wonder why these people came and the others wouldn't? . . .

I wonder how the master feels about the guests? . . .

I wonder how the guests feel about the master? . . .

I wonder how many could really be at this table? . . .

I wonder if you have ever been near a table like this? . . .

I wonder where this table might really be? . . .

Return to the weekly worship center order and continue. The scripture reading is Luke 14:15–24.

MATERIALS

1. Gold box
2. Green felt underlay, 36 by 36 inches, with corners rounded
3. *Host, mounted on poster board and laminated
4. *Table, banquet food, field, oxen, and wedding rings, mounted on poster board and laminated
5. *Guests—poor, blind, lame, and maimed—in groups, drawn so pieces will fit together like a puzzle when placed around the table, also mounted on poster board and laminated

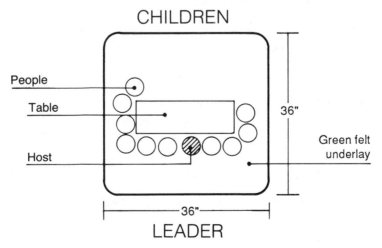

31

Lenten Puzzle

Turn to the liturgical shelf behind you and get the white satin cloth. Unfold it and smooth it out in front of you. Get the purple **Lenten Puzzle** *bag and place it in the center of the cloth. Sit quietly while you feel the story forming in you. Then run your hand over the bag.*

I wonder what this might be? It feels very rough. And it is purple . . . like the purple of Advent . . . when we were all getting ready for the birth of Jesus. Purple is the color for getting ready. . . . I wonder if there is something inside?

Carefully untie the bag, open it, and look in curiously.

Oh, look.

Bring out the pieces of the puzzle and lay them out, purple side up.

I wonder what these could be? They are rough too. And they are purple.

Touch each piece and count.

One, two, three, four, five, six . . . six purple pieces.

Sit back and wonder for a moment.

You know, today is the first Sunday in Lent. During Lent the church changes from the color green to the color purple.

Touch the purple bag and the puzzle pieces.

Lent is the time the church gets ready to celebrate the mystery of Easter. There are six Sundays in Lent for getting ready.

Touch the six pieces again.

I wonder if these six purple pieces can tell us what Lent is about?

Put the puzzle pieces together to form the cross.

Hmm. They form a cross.

Sit back and ponder a moment. Then place the pieces carefully, one by one, back into the bag and tie the cord.

> *Return to the weekly worship center order and continue. There is no scripture reading.*

MATERIALS

1. Bag, 9 by 12 inches, with gold drawstring, purple burlap lined with white satin so it can be turned inside out on Easter
2. Cross, cut into six pieces, purple and rough on one side, white and smooth on the other

CHILDREN

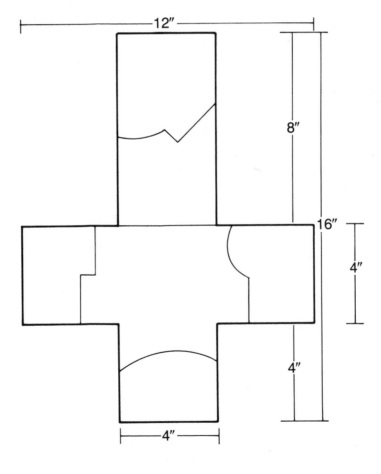

LEADER

32

Jesus and the Children
Matthew 19:13–15; Mark 10:13–16;
Luke 18:15–17

Walk slowly to the sacred story shelf and pick up the tray with the materials for Lent and the baskets for **Jesus and the Children.** *Carry them carefully with both hands to the circle and place them beside you. Sit quietly while you feel the story forming in you. Then roll out the purple underlay as you say:*

> This is the season of Lent . . . the time we get ready to celebrate the mystery of Easter . . . the time we are all on the way to Jerusalem. But who will show us the way? . . . Jesus shows us the way.

Roll out the beige road, smooth it, and place Jerusalem on its square at the end to your left as you say:

> Once every year the people of God go up to Jerusalem, the holy city of God, to celebrate the feast of the Passover, to remember how God led them through the waters to freedom. This year as Jesus traveled to Jerusalem . . .

Present Jesus and move him along the road a little.

> . . . crowds of people came to be close to him.

Take the two disciples and, starting from the corners of the underlay to your right, move them simultaneously to the road until they are touching Jesus.

> They came to hear him teach.

Move Jesus off the road onto the purple underlay just in front of you. Move the disciples to either side of Jesus.

> The little children wanted to come to Jesus too.

Move children onto the road from both your right and left and have them form a semicircle on the road facing Jesus.

But Jesus' disciples said:

Move disciples simultaneously toward the road in front of Jesus. Put disciples together, so they block the children, and say:

"No! Don't bother Jesus. He has important work to do."

Pause.

Then Jesus said, "Let the children come to me. Do not stop them, for to such belongs the Kingdom of God."

Turn the two disciples sideways so children can pass between them to Jesus. Move children to Jesus one at a time. Have Jesus take them in his arms and bless them. Position each so they form a semicircle, leaving the center open so you can move Jesus forward to the disciples.

Jesus said, "It is true. Anyone who will not receive the Kingdom of God like a little child will never enter it."

Responding to God's Word: Wondering Together

I wonder how the children felt on their way to see Jesus? . . .

I wonder how they felt when the disciples said, "No!"? . . .

I wonder what Jesus said to the children? . . .

I wonder what the children said to Jesus? . . .

I wonder what it was like to be close to Jesus? . . .

I wonder what it's like to receive the Kingdom of God like a child? . . .

Return to the weekly worship center order and continue. The scripture reading is Luke 18:15–17.

MATERIALS

1. Tray with materials for Lent:
   Purple felt underlay, 96 by 20 inches
   Beige felt road, 96 by 8 inches
   *Model of city of Jerusalem, with gateway
   *Model of city of Jericho (for sessions 33 and 34)
2. *Wooden figures of Jesus, two disciples, and six varied-size children
3. Two baskets for figures: 5-inch for Jesus and disciples, 6-inch for children

Diagram for Session 32 is found on p. 182 in Session 33.

33

Jesus and Bartimaeus
Matthew 20:29–34; Mark 10:46–52;
Luke 18:35–43

*Walk slowly to the sacred story shelf and pick up the tray with the materials for Lent and the tray with the **Bartimaeus** materials. Carry them carefully with both hands to the circle and place them beside you. Sit quietly while you feel the story forming in you. Then roll out the purple underlay as you say:*

This is the season of Lent . . . the time we get ready to celebrate the mystery of Easter . . . the time we are all on the way to Jerusalem. But who will show us the way? Jesus shows us the way.

Roll out the beige road, smooth it, and place Jerusalem on its square at the end to your left and Jericho in from the other end as you say:

Once every year the people of God go up to Jerusalem, the holy city of God, to celebrate the feast of the Passover, to remember how God led them through the water to freedom.

This year as Jesus traveled to Jerusalem, people came to him.

Place Jesus on the road.

They came to be close to him because they knew Jesus would not turn anyone away, even if they were little children . . .

Place a child close to Jesus.

. . . even if they were crippled or very poor . . .

Place next person close to Jesus.

. . . even if they were sick and scared, and no one would talk to them.

Place third person.

Bartimaeus . . .

Present Bartimaeus and place him along the road to your right of Jericho.

. . . was begging outside the city of Jericho. He was begging because he was blind. He couldn't see anything. But Bartimaeus could hear.

Move Jesus along the road.

When he heard Jesus going by he shouted, "Jesus, help me!"

Move Jesus on by. Move people toward Bartimaeus, blocking him from Jesus, and say:

The people said to Bartimaeus, "Be quiet. Don't bother Jesus. Be quiet!"

Move Jesus on slowly.

But Bartimaeus shouted louder, "Jesus, help me!" And Jesus stopped.

Stop Jesus and turn him toward Bartimaeus.

"Bring him to me," he said.

Take Bartimaeus to Jesus, leaving people there.

"What do you want?" Jesus asked.

Touch Jesus.

"I want to see."

Touch Bartimaeus' eyes.

"Then receive your sight!" Immediately Bartimaeus could see.

Bartimaeus and all the people were so happy they couldn't help but give thanks to God. And Bartimaeus followed Jesus, on the way . . . to Jerusalem.

Move Jesus along in front of Jericho and follow with Bartimaeus.

Responding to God's Word: Wondering Together

I wonder how it feels to be blind? . . .

I wonder how it feels to see for the very first time? . . .

I wonder why Jesus would listen to Bartimaeus when the others would just tell him to be quiet? . . .

I wonder why Jesus would come near Bartimaeus when others wouldn't bother with him? . . .

I wonder why the first thing Bartimaeus did after he could see was to follow Jesus on the way? . . .

I wonder how Bartimaeus felt following Jesus on the way to Jerusalem? . . .

Return to the weekly worship center order and continue. The scripture reading is Luke 18:35–43.

MATERIALS

1. Tray with materials for Lent
2. *Wooden figures of Jesus, Bartimaeus, woman, child, and man
3. Two five-inch baskets for figures
4. *Model of Jericho

Session 32

CHILDREN

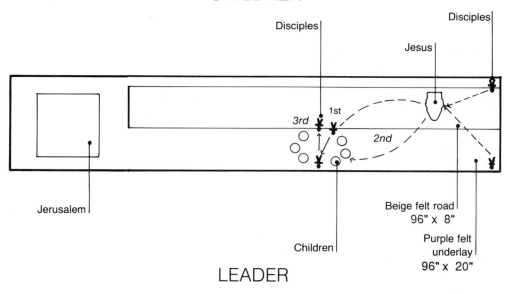

LEADER

Session 33

CHILDREN

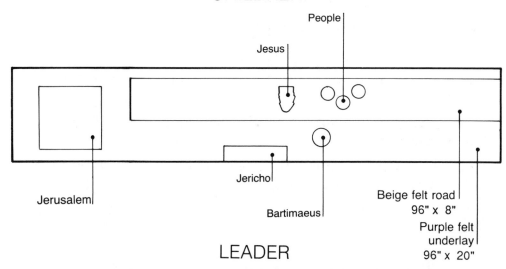

LEADER

34

Jesus and Zacchaeus
Luke 19:1–10

*Walk slowly to the sacred story shelf and pick up the tray with the materials for Lent and the baskets of **Zacchaeus** materials. Carry them carefully with both hands to the circle and place them beside you. Sit quietly while you feel the story forming in you. Then roll out the purple underlay as you say:*

This is the season of Lent . . . the time we get ready to celebrate the mystery of Easter . . . the time we are all on the way to Jerusalem. But who will show us the way? Jesus shows us the way.

Roll out the beige road, smooth it, and place Jerusalem on its square at the end to your left as you say:

Once every year the people of God go up to Jerusalem, the holy city of God, to celebrate the feast of the Passover, to remember how God led them through the waters to freedom. This year Jesus was going through the city of Jericho . . .

Place Jericho at the edge of the underlay near you and place the tree down the road to your left.

. . . on his way to Jerusalem. Crowds of people wanted to see him.

Place three people on the side of the road closer to you and three people opposite them.

Zacchaeus was the chief tax collector.

Present Zacchaeus.

People didn't like Zacchaeus. He took too much of their money. So he was very rich. Zacchaeus wanted to see Jesus too.

Put Zacchaeus behind the three people and move him up and down, trying to see over them.

But he was too short.

Show him trying to squeeze between them and move people close together so he can't.

183

And the people would not let him through. So Zacchaeus climbed a sycamore tree.

Move him behind the people and up into the tree.

When Jesus came . . .

Move Jesus along the road between the people and stop him beside the tree.

. . . he looked up . . . and called him . . . *by name.* "Zacchaeus, come down. I must stay with you today." Zacchaeus was so happy, he couldn't help but come right down.

Take him down and walk Jesus and Zacchaeus back along the road together.

But the people were angry.

Say the following as they walk between the people:

"Why is Jesus staying with Zacchaeus? Zacchaeus does bad things. He's a tax collector. He takes money that isn't his."

Move them off the road by Jericho and stop them, with Jesus and Zacchaeus facing each other and with Jesus' back to the crowd.

Then Zacchaeus said, "Jesus, I will give half of everything I have to the poor. And if I have taken money that doesn't belong to me, I will give it back and four times more."

Jesus said, "Zacchaeus, today you are saved. You are right with God, and you are right with people."

Turn Jesus toward the people and say:

"I, the special Son of God, have come to find and to save everyone who is lost."

Responding to God's Word: Wondering Together

I wonder what it is like to be so short that you can't see what you want to see? . . .

I wonder how Zacchaeus felt when Jesus called him by name? . . .

I wonder what Jesus and Zacchaeus said as they walked together? . . .

I wonder if it was hard for Zacchaeus to give back what didn't belong to him? . . .

I wonder how he felt when he gave half of his things to the poor? . . .

I wonder how the poor felt? . . .

I wonder how Zacchaeus felt when he was right with God and right with people? . . .

I wonder what Jesus meant when he said he came to find the lost? . . .

Return to the weekly worship center order and continue. The scripture reading is Luke 19:1–10.

MATERIALS

1. Tray with materials for Lent
2. *Wooden tree, model of Jericho
3. *Wooden figures of Jesus, Zacchaeus, and six people
4. Two baskets for figures: 5-inch for Jesus, Zacchaeus, and tree; 6-inch for people

CHILDREN

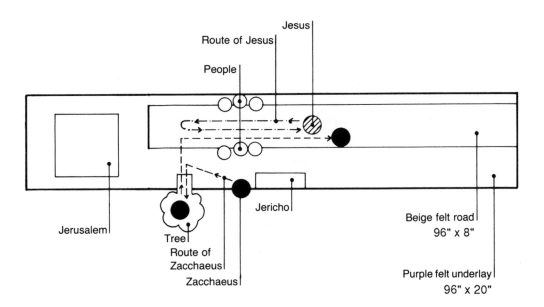

LEADER

35

Jesus the King
Matthew 21:1–11; Mark 11:1–11;
Luke 19:29–44; John 12:12–19

*Walk slowly to the sacred story shelf and pick up the tray with the **Jesus the King** materials. Carry it carefully with both hands to the circle and place it beside you. Sit quietly while you feel the story forming in you. Then roll out the purple underlay as you say:*

This is the season of Lent . . . the time we get ready to celebrate the mystery of Easter . . . the time we are all on the way to Jerusalem. But who will show us the way? Jesus shows us the way.

Roll out the beige road, smooth it, and place Jerusalem on its square at the end to your left as you say:

Once every year the people of God go up to Jerusalem, to celebrate the feast of the Passover, to remember how God led them through the water to freedom.

This year as Jesus traveled to Jerusalem . . .

Present Jesus on the donkey and move him along the road.

. . . people hoped he would be their *king*. When they heard Jesus was near Jerusalem, they ran to him and shouted, "Blessed is the *King* who comes in the name of the Lord!" They put their cloaks and palm branches on the road to prepare a way for Jesus and shouted:

Place a "purple cloak" on the road, using a motion like spreading a table-cloth, and say:

"Hosanna in the highest!"

Place palms on the cloak and say:

"Blessed is he who comes in the name of the Lord!"

Continue doing this in rhythm. The road will be made through the gate of Jerusalem and will be built with four "purple cloaks" spread out on "Hosanna in the highest!" The palms will be placed on "Blessed is he . . . ." (These words are part of the Great Prayer of Thanksgiving.)

Hosanna in the highest!

Blessed is he who comes in the name of the Lord!

Hosanna in the highest!

Blessed is he who comes in the name of the Lord!

Hosanna in the highest!

Blessed is he who comes in the name of the Lord!

You can prepare the way for Jesus the King. When it is your turn you may come and choose a cloak and palms to put on the road too.

The children may choose a "cloak" from a variety of colors and textures. (They say spontaneously, "Hosanna," etc.) After they have built the road, place your own "cloak" and palms. Then move Jesus over them and through the gate to Jerusalem, while all say:

Hosanna in the highest!

Blessed is he who comes in the name of the Lord!

Hosanna in the highest!

Responding to God's Word: Wondering Together

I wonder how Jesus felt when the crowd wanted him to be their king? . . .

I wonder who the people were who shouted, "Blessed is he who comes in the name of the Lord"? . . .

I wonder why Jesus the King rode on a donkey instead of a horse? . . .

I wonder what kind of king Jesus would be? . . .

I wonder what it would be like to live in Jesus' kingdom? . . .

Return to the weekly worship center order and continue. The scripture reading is John 12:12–13.

MATERIALS

1. Tray with materials for Lent
2. *Wooden figure of Jesus on a donkey
3. Four purple "cloaks," 5 by 8 inches, to spread on the road
4. One "cloak" for each child and yourself, made from different kinds and colors of cloth, each 3 by 4 inches
5. Silk palm leaves, enough for each child and yourself to have two

6. Two 6-inch baskets, one for "cloaks," one for palm leaves (could use lids of other baskets)

CHILDREN

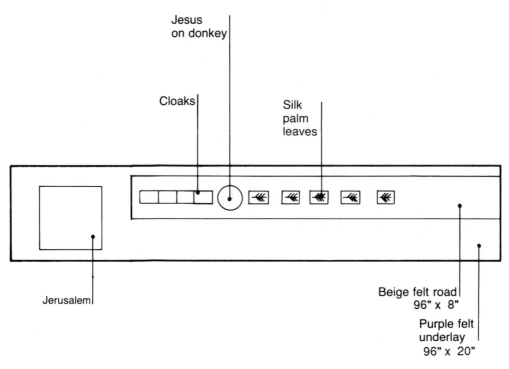

LEADER

36

Jesus' Last Passover
Matthew 26:26–28

Walk slowly to the sacred story shelf and pick up the tray with the materials for **Jesus' Last Passover.** *Carry it carefully with both hands to the circle and place it beside you. Sit quietly while you feel the story forming in you. Then roll out the green felt underlay and smooth it, as you say:*

Once every year, the people of God . . .

Place the disciples on the underlay so they are in three rows, four figures abreast, as you slowly continue:

. . . go up to Jerusalem . . . to celebrate the feast . . . of the Passover . . . to remember how God led them . . . through the waters to freedom. Every year Jesus . . .

Present Jesus and place him to your right, facing the disciples, so they block his movement.

. . . celebrated the Passover feast in Jerusalem with his family and friends.

Motion over the heads of the disciples.

But this year Jesus' friends did not want to go. They were afraid. They said to Jesus, "Don't go. People in Jerusalem want to kill you."

Pause.

But Jesus said, "We must go."

Move Jesus toward you and around the disciples, stopping him about six inches before you get to the space where the backdrop will go. So that you will only have to move three pairs of disciples, move two from each of the ends closest to you so they are lined up behind Jesus in twos.

When the day of Passover came, some of Jesus' friends went to an upper room . . .

Place the upper room backdrop near the end of the underlay to your left.

. . . and prepared the feast.

Place the table in front of the backdrop. Put the plate with unleavened bread (plasticene) on the table and then the cup.

When evening came, Jesus . . .

Move Jesus to the upper room by going in front of the table and then around to the center back. Follow with the disciples as you say:

. . . and his friends went to the upper room to celebrate the feast of Passover. They were still afraid.

When all are around the table, say:

Then Jesus . . .

Touch Jesus.

. . . said the words of the feast in a way they had never heard before. Jesus *took* the bread . . .

With both hands, lift the bread straight up and hold it.

. . . and *blessed* it . . .

Place your hand over it like a blessing.

. . . and *broke* it . . .

Break it in two.

. . . and *gave* it to them, saying,

As you lower your hands with the broken bread, reach out to the two disciples facing Jesus and offer it to them, as you say:

"Take. Eat. This is my body, broken for you."

Continue around the circle as you say this. Then place the bread on the plate.

Then Jesus took the cup . . .

Lift the cup straight up with two hands.

. . . and said, "Drink this, all of you. This is my blood which is shed for you."

Lower the cup and pass it to each disciple. Pause and sit back. Then say:

Then they sang a hymn and went out to a garden to pray.

Move Jesus and disciples out, behind the backdrop so they can't be seen.

Then it happened. People who didn't like Jesus took him. They wouldn't let him go. Later they nailed him to a cross to kill him. . . . Jesus died. It was very sad. . . .

Pause for a moment.

But three days later God did an amazing thing. God made Jesus alive again.

Pause for a moment and look at the table.

So, every time we eat this bread . . .

Touch the bread.

. . . and drink this cup . . .

Touch the cup.

. . . we remember Jesus, and that God made him alive again.

Responding to God's Word: Wondering Together

I wonder how it felt to be around this table and to hear Jesus say, "Take. Eat. This is my body broken for you"? . . .

I wonder how the disciples felt eating the bread and drinking the wine? . . .

I wonder how they felt when Jesus died? . . .

I wonder how they felt when they heard God made Jesus alive? . . .

I wonder if you have ever been close to a table like this? . . .

> *Return to the weekly worship center order and continue. The scripture reading is Matthew 26:26–28.*

MATERIALS

1. Green underlay, 18 by 48 inches
2. *Wooden figures of Jesus and twelve disciples
3. *Wooden table 3 by 8½ by 2 inches high
4. Basket for figures (7-inch)
5. Backdrop of upper room: center part, 7 by 14 inches; each end, 7 by 4 inches
6. Small plate with plasticene loaf of unleavened bread
7. Small chalice
8. Basket (2½- to 3-inch) for plate, chalice, and bread
9. Tray for materials

CHILDREN

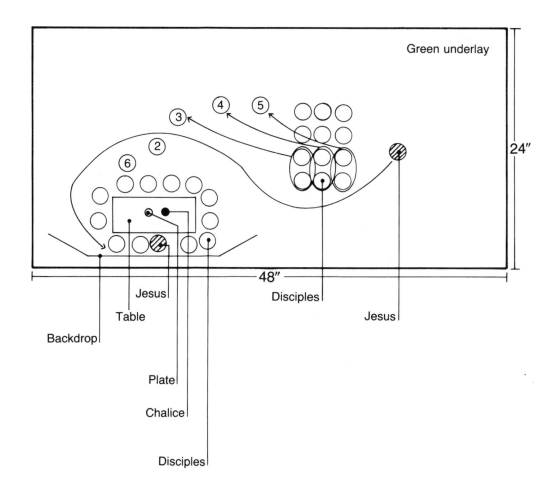

Green underlay

24″

48″

Jesus

Table

Backdrop

Plate

Chalice

Disciples

Disciples

Jesus

LEADER

37

Jesus Is Risen:
Appearance to Mary Magdalene
Matthew 27:57–28:10; John 20:1–18

Walk slowly to the sacred story shelf and pick up the tray with the materials for **Jesus' Appearance to Mary.** *Carry it carefully with two hands to the circle and place it beside you. Sit quietly while you feel the story forming in you. Then roll out the white underlay and smooth it as you say:*

Today is Easter, the day we celebrate the mystery that Jesus died and that God made him alive again.

Roll out the beige road. Then take the tomb and place it near the edge of the underlay near you and say:

This is a tomb. It is a special place for the dead.

Place the stone in front of the opening.

When Jesus died, his friends took his body from the cross and put it here.

Move your hand over the surface of the tomb.

They rolled a huge stone in front to close it.

Trace the stone with your finger. Pause. Take the angel and silently roll the stone away. Put the angel behind the stone. Then present Mary and place her on the road.

Mary Magdalene loved Jesus very much. So early Sunday morning, Mary and her friends went back to the tomb.

Place her friends beside her and begin moving them toward the tomb.

The tomb was open. Jesus was gone. "Where is he?" they cried.

Bring the angel out from behind the stone.

Then the angel said, "Don't be afraid. Be joyful. Jesus is alive! Go tell the disciples Jesus is risen from the dead."

Move Mary's friends away from the tomb and along the road. Leave Mary near the tomb.

But Mary Magdalene would not leave. She stood crying.

Move Jesus toward her back.

Then someone said, "Who are you looking for?" . . .

Turn Mary around.

. . . and he called her by name: "Mary!" She knew the sound of his voice. It was Jesus! Jesus was alive!

Mary Magdalene was so happy she couldn't help but tell Jesus' friends.

Move Mary to the others.

"I have seen the Lord. Jesus is risen! The Lord is risen indeed."

Responding to God's Word: Wondering Together

I wonder what it was like to be going to Jesus' tomb that Sunday morning? . . .

I wonder how Mary felt when Jesus died? . . .

I wonder what it feels like when someone or something you love dies? . . .

I wonder how Mary felt when Jesus' body was not in the tomb? . . .

I wonder what it was like to hear, "Jesus is alive. Jesus is risen"? . . .

I wonder how Mary knew this person was Jesus? . . .

I wonder how Mary felt when Jesus called her by name? . . .

I wonder what it felt like to tell others that Jesus is risen? . . .

I wonder how we can know that Jesus is alive? . . .

Return to the weekly worship center order and continue. The scripture reading is John 20:11–18.

MATERIALS

1. White felt underlay, 34 by 36 inches, with corners rounded
2. Beige felt for road, 30 inches long by 4 inches wide
3. Tomb, made from gray clay, large enough to put Jesus figure in (while putting Jesus in the tomb isn't in the story, the children do this when using the materials)
4. Stone to roll in front of tomb, made from gray clay
5. *Wooden figures of Mary, two women, angel, and risen Jesus

6. Two 5-inch baskets for figures: one for Mary and women, one for angel and Jesus
7. Tray for materials

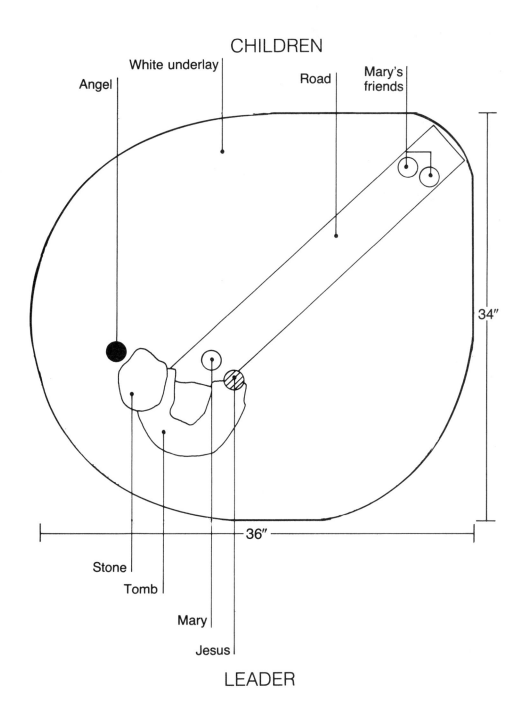

38

Jesus Is Risen:
The Road to Emmaus

Luke 24:1–35

Walk slowly to the sacred story shelf and get the tray with the **Emmaus** *materials. Carry it carefully with both hands to the circle and place it beside you. Sit quietly while you feel the story forming in you. Then roll out the white underlay and smooth it as you say:*

This is the season of Easter, when we celebrate the mystery that Jesus died and that God made him alive again.

Roll out the beige road as you say:

This is the road from Jerusalem to Emmaus.

Place the backdrop and the table alongside the road at the end to your right.

Two of Jesus' friends were going down to Emmaus.

Present them and move them along the road.

They were very sad. Jesus had died. They had hoped he would be king. "Why did Jesus have to die?" they said. "Why did Jesus die?" . . . Then someone came and walked with them.

Place Jesus between them and keep moving to the house.

He told them why Jesus died.

When they reach the house, say:

"Stay with us," they said.

Place Jesus behind the table and the two men across the table from him. Then place a plate with a loaf of bread and a chalice on the table.

The man *took* the bread . . .

Pick up the loaf with the fingers of both hands and elevate it. Use the same motions as in **Jesus' Last Passover.**

. . . and *blessed* it . . .

Make a sign of blessing.

196

. . . and *broke* it . . .

Break the bread in half.

. . . and *gave* it to them.

Offer the bread to each.

Then they knew who he was. He was Jesus. Jesus was alive! Jesus was risen from the dead!

Pause.

Then Jesus left.

Move Jesus behind the backdrop.

They were so happy that Jesus was alive, they couldn't help but go back to Jerusalem and tell the disciples.

Move them to Jerusalem.

"Jesus is alive! He is risen! The Lord is risen indeed!"

Responding to God's Word: Wondering Together

I wonder how Jesus' friends felt when Jesus died? . . .

I wonder how they knew Jesus was alive? Or how they knew the person was Jesus? . . .

I wonder what it felt like to recognize Jesus in the breaking of the bread? . . .

I wonder if you have ever been close to bread like this? . . .

I wonder how it feels to know Jesus is alive? . . .

I wonder what it was like to tell others that Jesus is alive? . . .

Return to the weekly worship center order and continue. The scripture reading is Luke 24:28–35.

MATERIALS

1. White felt underlay, 24 by 45 inches
2. Beige felt road, 6 by 45 inches
3. Backdrop for house at Emmaus: center, 5½ inches high by 7 inches wide; ends, each 5½ inches high by 2½ inches wide
4. *Wooden figures of two disciples and risen Jesus
5. Basket for wooden figures (5-inch)
6. Wooden table, 3 by 5 inches and 2 inches high

7. Small plate with plasticene bread
8. Small chalice
8. Basket for plate, bread, and chalice (2½- to 3-inch)
9. Tray for materials

CHILDREN

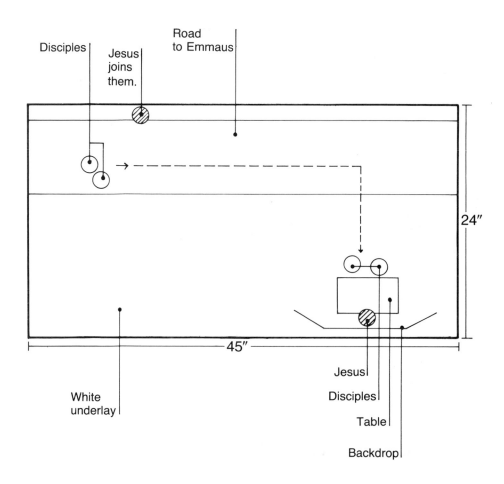

LEADER

39

The Good Shepherd
and the Wolf
Psalm 23; John 10; Matthew 18

For this session, repeat the actions and words of Session 5, **The Good Shepherd,** *to the point where the shepherd moves safely through the rocks. Refer to the diagram on page 86. Then pick up as follows:*

Move the sheep through, losing one in the rocks.

"I count each one of my sheep as they go inside.

Point silently to each sheep. Pause and point to the empty space.

And if any is missing, I would go anywhere to look for the lost sheep:

Slowly move the Good Shepherd through the grass, by the water, and stop in the rocks.

Through the green grass . . . by the still water . . . calling my sheep by name, even in places of danger. And when I find the lost sheep, I carry it home . . .

Place the sheep on the Good Shepherd and continue moving through the places of danger.

. . . even if it is very heavy, . . . even if I am very tired.

Place the sheep in the sheepfold and close the gate.

When all my sheep are safe inside, I'm so happy. . . . But I can't be happy all by myself, so I call all my friends, and we have a great feast."

Pause. Move the Good Shepherd back alongside the sheepfold. Take out the ordinary shepherd.

This is the ordinary shepherd. When the ordinary shepherd takes the sheep from the sheepfold . . . the ordinary shepherd does not walk in front of the sheep to show them the way. So the sheep wander and scatter.

Move the sheep off in all directions.

When the wolf comes . . .

Take the wolf from the box and, in a sweeping motion, move it to the rocks.

. . . the ordinary shepherd runs away.

Move the ordinary shepherd across the underlay toward the lower left and then return him to the box out of sight.

But the Good Shepherd . . .

Move the Good Shepherd between the wolf and the sheep.

. . . stands between the wolf and the sheep and even gives his life for the sheep . . . so the sheep can return safely home.

Slide each sheep into the sheepfold and close the gate. Place the wolf back in the box out of sight. Move the Good Shepherd alongside the sheepfold. Pause. Sit back.

Responding to God's Word: Wondering Together

I wonder if the sheep have names? . . .

I wonder if the sheep are happy in this place? . . .

Trace the sheepfold with your finger.

I wonder how many sheep really could live in this place? . . .

I wonder if you have ever had to go through places of danger or were lost and someone found you? . . .

I wonder if the wolf has ever been close to you? . . .

I wonder if you have ever heard the Good Shepherd say your name?

Trace the shape of the sheepfold.

I wonder where this place might really be? . . .

Trace the outline of the whole underlay.

I wonder where this whole place might really be? . . .

Return to the weekly worship center order and continue. The scripture reading is John 10:11–16.

MATERIALS

1. Parable box from Session 5
2. Laminated ordinary shepherd
3. Laminated wolf

40

The Good Shepherd
and the Lord's Supper (I)
Psalm 23; John 10; Matthew 18

Walk slowly to the liturgical shelf and get the **Good Shepherd and the Lord's Supper** *tray. Carry it to the circle. Place the circle with the table next to the circle with the sheepfold, making sure they touch at one point. Silently touch the connecting point of the two circles for a moment. Sit quietly while you feel the story forming in you. Then say:*

Once there was someone who said such amazing things and did such wonderful things that people began to follow him. But they didn't know who he was. So one day they simply had to ask him, and he said, "I am the Good Shepherd.

Touch the Good Shepherd.

I know each one of my sheep by name.

Touch each sheep with a gentle stroking.

And they know the sound of my voice. So when I call my sheep from the sheepfold, they follow me.

Open the gate. Begin to move the Good Shepherd out from the door with the sheep following.

I walk in front of the sheep to show them the way.

Continue moving the sheep, with the Good Shepherd leading the way, around the edge of the circle toward the point where the two circles touch. Do not hurry. There is a great deal of silence. Move the Good Shepherd, and then go back and move each sheep along. When the Shepherd and the sheep move across the point of contact between the circles, pause a second before crossing.

I show them the way to the good green grass."

Bring the Shepherd and the sheep around the front of the table, moving them on the outer edge of the circle. When the sheep are all around the table, move the Shepherd forward. Then trace the edges of the table as you say:

This is the table of the Good Shepherd.

Open the basket with the plate and bread, present them, and place them on the table.

A special plate . . .

Pick up the cup and present it. Then put it on the table as you say:

. . . and a special cup are on this table. Here the Good Shepherd feeds his sheep.

Gesture toward the table. Pause. Sit back a moment.

Responding to God's Word: Wondering Together

I wonder if these sheep have names? . . .

I wonder if the sheep are happy to be at this great feast? . . .

I wonder if you have ever been close to this table? . . .

Point to the table.

I wonder if you have ever felt the Good Shepherd there with you? . . .

I wonder if you have ever heard the very words of the Good Shepherd? . . .

I wonder how many sheep can come to this table? . . .

I wonder where they come from? Look. . . .

Trace the movement from the sheepfold around the first circle and then around the second circle.

I wonder where this whole place might really be? . . .

> *Return to the weekly worship center order and continue. The scripture reading is John 10:2–4.*

MATERIALS

1. *Two wooden circles, cut from ¼-inch plywood and covered with green felt, 13 inches in diameter (see plans). On the first circle, make a "sheepfold" from dowels with two rows of string strung between like a fence; one section is a gate. On the second circle place a small table, 4 by 8 by 2 inches high.
2. Small chalice
3. Small plate with clay bread or wafer
4. Basket for chalice, plate, and bread (2½ to 3 inches)
5. *Wooden figure of the Good Shepherd

6. *Wooden figures of ten sheep
7. Basket for the sheep (5-inch)
8. *Wooden figures of five adults—one is a pastor—and five children
9. Basket for the people (7-inch)
10. Tray for materials

CHILDREN

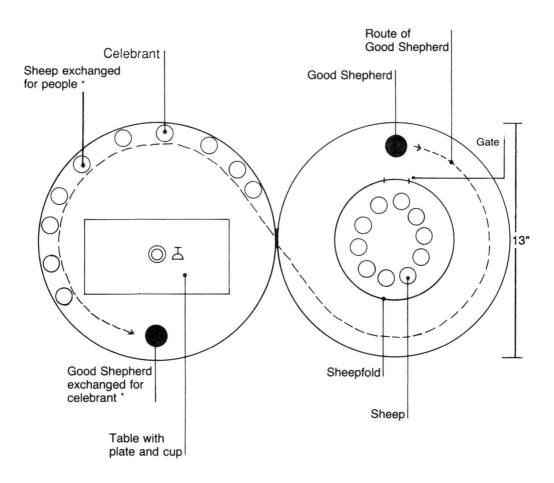

*In Session 41

LEADER

41

The Good Shepherd
and the Lord's Supper (II)
1 Corinthians 11:23–26

Walk slowly to the liturgical shelf and get the **Good Shepherd and the Lord's Supper** *tray. Carry it to the circle. Place the circle with the table next to the circle with the sheepfold, making sure they touch at one point. Silently touch the connecting point of the two circles for a moment. Sit quietly while you feel the story forming in you. Then say:*

Once there was someone who said such amazing things and did such wonderful things that people began to follow him. But they didn't know who he was. So one day they simply had to ask him, and he said, "I am the Good Shepherd.

Touch the Good Shepherd.

I know each one of my sheep by name.

Touch each sheep with a gentle stroking.

And they know the sound of my voice. So when I call my sheep from the sheepfold, they follow me.

Open the gate. Begin to move the Good Shepherd out from the door with the sheep following.

I walk in front of the sheep to show them the way.

Continue moving the sheep, with the Good Shepherd leading the way, around the edge of the circle toward the point where the two circles touch. Do not hurry. There is a great deal of silence. Move the Good Shepherd, and then go back and move each sheep along. When the Shepherd and the sheep move across the point of contact between the circles, pause a second before crossing.

I show them the way to the good green grass."

Bring the Shepherd and the sheep around the front of the table, moving them on the outer edge of the circle. When the sheep are all around the table, move the Shepherd forward. Then trace the edges of the table as you say:

This is the table of the Good Shepherd.

Open the basket with the plate and bread, present them, and place them on the table.

A special plate . . .

Pick up the cup and present it. Then put it on the table as you say:

. . . and a special cup are on this table. Here the Good Shepherd feeds his sheep.

Gesture toward the table. Pause. Sit back a moment.

Many come to this joyful feast. They come from east . . .

Present an adult figure and exchange it for a sheep from the left side of the table.

. . . and west . . .

Present another adult figure and exchange it for a sheep from the right side of the table.

. . . and from north and south.

Present the figure of the celebrant (pastor) and exchange it for the sheep opposite the Good Shepherd. Continue replacing every other sheep.

Pick up a child and present it and say:

And the children come too.

Place the children between the adults. Pause a moment. Then remove the Good Shepherd figure, placing it in the basket.

The Good Shepherd is still with us, in the holy bread and the holy wine.

Elevate each as you name them.

And one of the people of God . . .

Pick up the celebrant, who is opposite the Good Shepherd at the table, and bring to the place where the Shepherd was.

. . . called a celebrant, comes and says the very words of the Good Shepherd . . . and all share in his presence here.

Motion around the circle of people, bringing your hands to point to the bread and wine. Sit back in silence for a moment.

Responding to God's Word: Wondering Together

I wonder if these people have names? . . .

I wonder if the people are happy to be at this great feast? . . .

I wonder where this place might really be? . . .

Point to the table.

I wonder if you have ever been close to this table? . . .

I wonder if you have ever felt the Good Shepherd there with you? . . .

I wonder if you have ever heard the very words of the Good Shepherd? . . .

I wonder how many people can come to this table? . . .

I wonder where they come from? Look. . . .

Trace the movement from the sheepfold around the first circle and then around the second circle.

I wonder where this whole place might really be? . . .

Return to the weekly worship center order and continue. The scripture reading is I Corinthians 11:23–26.

42

Ascension

Luke 24:44–53; John 14–17; Acts 1:1–11

Walk slowly to the liturgical shelf and pick up the tray with the **Ascension** *materials. Carry it carefully with both hands to the circle and place it beside you. Roll out the white satin underlay as you say:*

This is the season of Easter, when we celebrate the mystery that Jesus died and that God made him alive again.

Continue to smooth out the underlay gently and slowly as you continue:

Today is Ascension Day [or Sunday], when we celebrate another mystery . . . the mystery that Jesus went away so he could be with us always . . . in every place and . . . every time.

The Christ candle helps us remember the mystery of Easter.

Place the Christ candle on the white satin underlay. Touch the wick and move your hands down the candle.

When there is no light, we say, "Christ has died." But Jesus is alive. God raised Jesus . . .

Move hands slowly back up the candle.

. . . from the dead, so we say, "Christ is risen."

Light the candle as you say "Christ is risen" and enjoy the light for a while. Then point to the flame and say slowly and with an air of mystery:

Jesus was alive again. One day he said to his friends, "Stay in Jerusalem. God will send you a special gift . . . the gift of the Holy Spirit. The Holy Spirit will give you power . . . power to tell everyone about me and the Kingdom of God.

I am going away. You will not see me anymore. But I will be with you always . . . in every place and every time. . . . And I will come again. Then Jesus disappeared . . . into a cloud."

Place snuffer over the flame. Then, as you say "into a cloud," lift the snuffer slowly, as far as you can reach in the air, keeping your eyes on the smoke.

Keep looking up, with snuffer extended, as you say:

Hmm. This is the mystery of Ascension. Jesus went away, but somehow he is still with us.

Slowly lower the snuffer and look toward the candle as you say:

And "Christ will come again." Hmm. "Christ has died."

Say this wonderingly. Touch the wick and move your hands down the candle and pause. Then move your hands up the candle slowly and light the candle and say:

"Christ is risen."

Pause for a while. Then silently snuff the candle as you did before. Pause again. Then slowly bring the snuffer down as you say:

"Christ will come again." . . . This is the mystery of Easter.

Responding to God's Word: Wondering Together

I wonder how Jesus' friends felt when Jesus went away? . . .

I wonder if they kept looking for Jesus? . . .

I wonder how they knew Jesus was still with them? . . .

I wonder how they felt when Jesus told them God would give them the special gift of the Holy Spirit? . . .

I wonder what they will do with that gift? . . .

Return to the weekly worship center order and continue. The scripture reading is Acts 1:8–11.

MATERIALS

1. White satin underlay, 18 by 33 inches
2. The Christ candle, a large white candle with a wide base
3. Matches in a covered glass container
4. Candle snuffer

43

Pentecost
Acts 2

*Walk slowly to the shelf and pick up the tray with the **Pentecost** materials. Carry it carefully with both hands to the circle and place it beside you. Take out the red felt underlay and unroll and smooth it as you say:*

Today is the day of Pentecost, when we remember how God gave us the gift of the Holy Spirit so we can say and do the wonderful things that Jesus did.

It happened after Jesus went away. The people of God were in Jerusalem . . . to celebrate the great thanksgiving feast called Pentecost. They came from every country.

Place people in groups as follows: Starting from the left corner near you, move the mother and child figures simultaneously away from you, center left. Follow with the father. From the right corner near you, move the father and son figures together away from you, center right. From the far left corner, move two adult figures to the left of the first group. From the far right, move two adult figures. All figures should face one another slightly and form a semicircle, similar to the way you set out the animals around the Ark.

Pause and place the table at the center edge of the underlay near you and say:

Jesus' friends were in Jerusalem too.

Set Jesus' five friends around the table, with Peter at the center, behind the table, one at each end, and two in front as you say:

They were still waiting for the gift God promised to send, the gift of the Holy Spirit.

Pause.

Suddenly a sound like a mighty wind filled the whole room.

Move hand in a circular motion above the table, like a tornado funnel, with palm facing down.

And what looked like flames of fire . . .

Put both hands together with fingers tucked in. Explode them up as a fire, keeping heels of hands together and fingers apart like flames.

. . . came to rest on them. All were filled with the Holy Spirit.

Starting with the figure to your right, move around the table, making the shape of a flame with your thumb and forefinger as you touch each head.

They were so excited. They began to tell the amazing things God did.

Move the two persons from the front of the table to the groups in front of them.

They told about Jesus . . .

Move the figure at the right side of the table to the group opposite.

and that God raised Jesus from the dead.

Move the figure at the left side of the table to the group opposite.

The people from all the different countries could understand them.

Point to each group.

They heard in their own language. "What should we do?" they asked. Peter said . . .

Move Peter around to the front of the table.

. . . "Change your ways. . . . Be baptized. . . .

Cup your hand over their heads in a baptizing motion, beginning with the group to your right.

. . . You will be washed . . .

Cup your hands over the next group.

. . . clean . . .

Cup your hands over the next group.

. . . and new. And you will receive the Holy Spirit.

Starting with the group to your right, touch the forehead of each figure with the flame gesture you did above. Touch the children when you say "and for your children." Then finish with the adults.

God's promise is for you . . . and for your children, and for everyone God calls."

With hands together, extend arms forward and separate in a semicircle.

Responding to God's Word: Wondering Together

I wonder what it felt like to receive the gift of the Holy Spirit on Pentecost? . . .

I wonder how Jesus' friends felt as they told the amazing things about God? . . .

I wonder how the people felt when they where baptized and received the Holy Spirit? . . .

I wonder how they knew this was the Holy Spirit? . . .

I wonder what all these people will do now that they have the gift of the Holy Spirit? . . .

I wonder what it was like on the day you were baptized and received the Holy Spirit? . . .

I wonder what the Holy Spirit wants us to do with God's gifts? . . .

Today, during the feast, talk about the birthday of the church. Have a cake with a candle for each child on it. Mention that the candles remind us of the flames of the Holy Spirit at Pentecost.

> *Return to the weekly worship center order and continue. The scripture reading is Acts 2:1–4.*

MATERIALS

1. Red felt underlay, 24 by 36 inches
2. Table (as in upper room), 3 by 8½ by 2 inches high
3. *Twelve wooden adult figures—five of Jesus' friends and seven from other countries—and two children
4. Two baskets, one for the disciples (6-inch) and one for visitors and children (7-inch)
5. Tray for materials

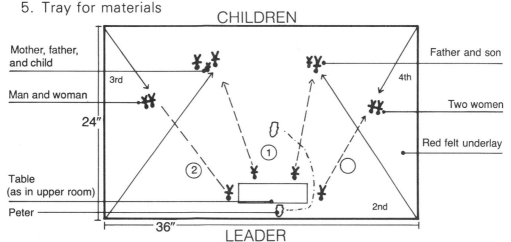

44

Baptism
Matthew 28:18–20; John 8:12; Acts 2:38–39

*Turn to the liturgical shelf behind you and get the white satin underlay. Unfold it and smooth it out in front of you. Get the Christ candle and place it in the center of the cloth. Then get the tray with the smaller white candles, the matches, and the candle snuffer. Get the **Baptism** materials also. Hide the matches in your hand. Sit quietly while you feel the story forming in you. Then say:*

Once there was someone who said such amazing things and did such wonderful things that people began to follow him. But they didn't know who he was. So one day they simply had to ask him. And he said, "I am the Light."

When you say the word "light," strike the match and light the Christ candle.

Let's enjoy the Light.

Sit peacefully and enjoy the light.

People who love the Light can become one with the Light. This is how your light becomes one with the Light. Watch.

Hold up one of the small candles and look at it. Then look at the child opposite you and say:

*[Name], this is your light.

Light the child's candle from the Christ candle and place it in a candle holder on the white underlay in front of the Christ candle, opposite the child. You will continue lighting candles for the rest of the group, alternating to the left and right of the center child so a semicircle is formed around the Christ candle representative of where each child is sitting. [You need to start opposite you and place the candles from the center so you will not be burned while reaching over candles. WARNING: You must be careful to reach around the Christ candle so you will not be burned or catch your clothing or hair on fire.]

Now take another candle and hold it up toward the next child. Look at the child and say:

[Name], this is your light.

Light the candle, put it in a holder, and place it next to the first candle. Alternating from both sides of the center child, continue lighting candles for each child, placing them in holders, forming a semicircle around the Christ candle. When several candles are lit, say:

Look how the light is growing. It all came from the Light here.

Point to the Light.

Look, the light is in so many places at once.

After lighting more candles, say:

Many have come to the Light to receive their light. But the Light is not smaller. It is still the same. . . . I wonder how so much light could be given away and the Light still be the same?

When all the children have a candle lighted for them, light one for yourself and say:

There was even a day when I received my light and become one with the Light. Let's enjoy the light.

Sit silently and enjoy the light.

There comes a time when the Light is changed so it's not just in one place anymore. It can be in many places at once. Watch. You see the light is just in one place now.

Point to the flame in your candle.

I'm going to change the light so it is not just in one place anymore. It can be in many places all at once. Watch.

Slowly lower the candle snuffer over your light, holding it over the wick a moment and then slowly raising it. Watch the smoke curl up into the air and fade into the whole room.

Now I will change your light so it can be in more than one place.

Change the light of each child. When all the lights are changed, change the Light as you say:

Even the Light was changed. The Light that was just in one place at one time is in all places in all times. So the Light can be everywhere in this room, and even in other places.

Sit silently for a moment and then slowly put everything back on the shelf except the **Baptism** *materials.*

Now the day that you received your light may have been a day when you were very tiny. Or it may be a day when you are grown big. When that happens, something is done in the church called baptism.

Place the "baptismal bowl" in front of you.

The mother and father and other people bring the little baby to the church.

Pick up the doll dressed in a white gown and cuddle it.

Then the pastor [priest] calls the baby by name and puts special water, the holy water, on the baby . . .

Put your hand into the water and put it on the doll's head. (Do this the way it is done in your church.)

. . . and says the special words, "I baptize you in the name of the Father, and the Son, and the Holy Spirit." And that is what happens on the day you receive your light. It is the day you come into the family of families we call the church.

Responding to God's Word: Wondering Together

Now I wonder what it was like on the day you received your light? . . .

I wonder what you were doing on the day you received your light? . . . *or* I wonder what it will be like on the day of your baptism? . . .

Return to the weekly worship center order and continue. The scripture reading is Acts 2:38–39 or Matthew 28:18–20.

MATERIALS

1. White satin underlay, 24 by 36 inches
2. The Christ candle, a large white candle with a wide base
3. Enough small white candles and candle holders for each person in the room
4. Matches in a covered glass container
5. Candle snuffer
6. Infant doll in a white gown
7. A beautiful small "baptismal bowl"
8. Tray for doll and bowl

PART IV

PATTERNS AND INSTRUCTIONS

Ordinary shepherd
(use with Session 39)

Good shepherd

Sheep (make 5)

Wolf

Session 7

Creation Cards

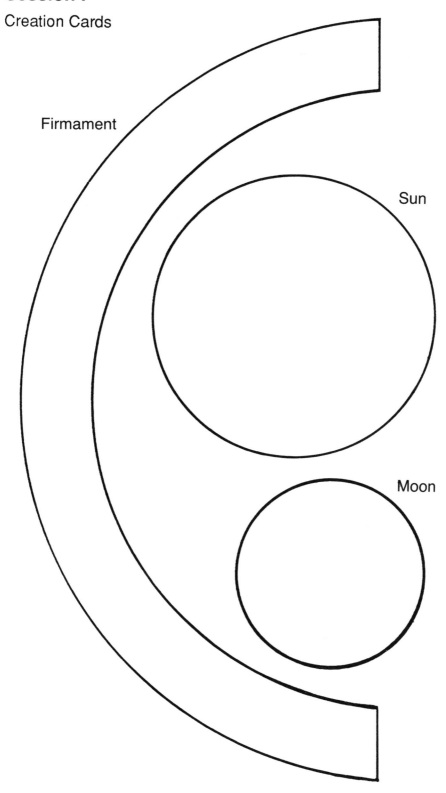

Firmament

Sun

Moon

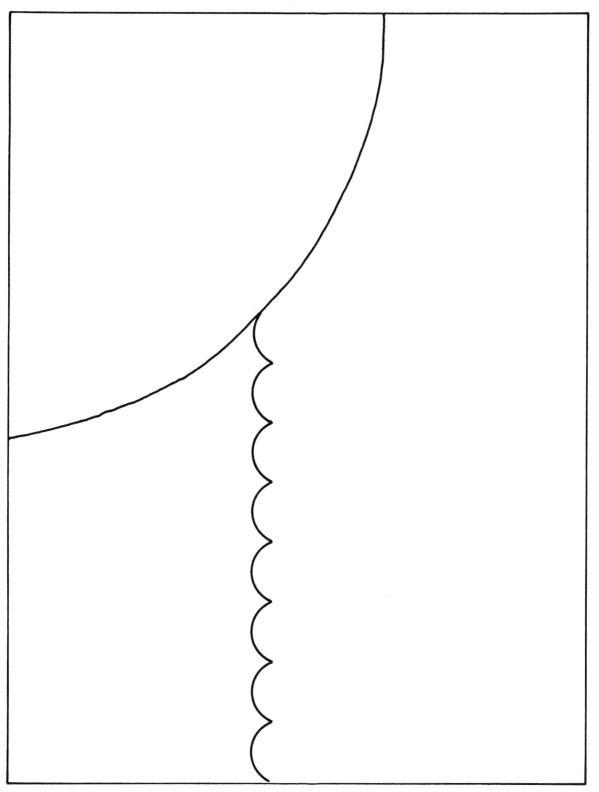

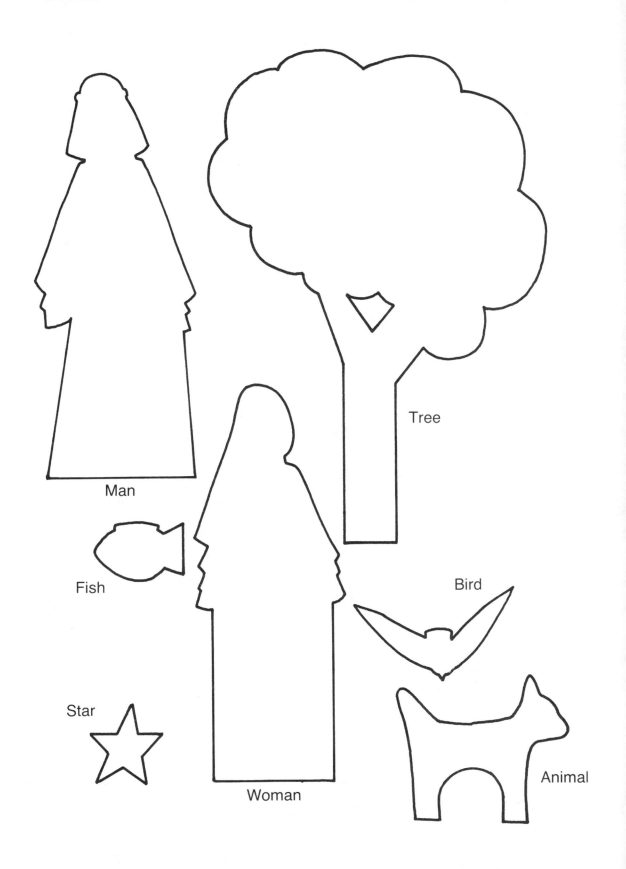

Tree

Man

Fish

Bird

Star

Woman

Animal

Session 9

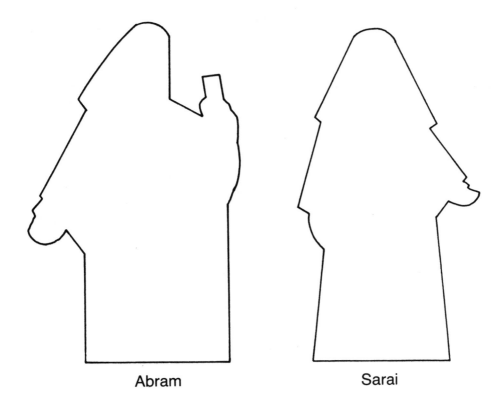

Abram

Sarai

Sessions 10 and 11

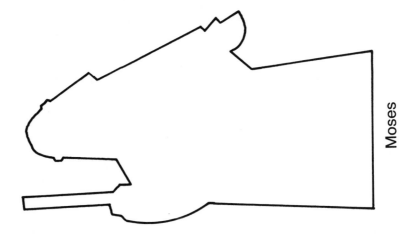

Moses

Cut this figure so the wood grain runs vertically.

People of God

Session 10
(also for Sessions 11, 13, and 15)

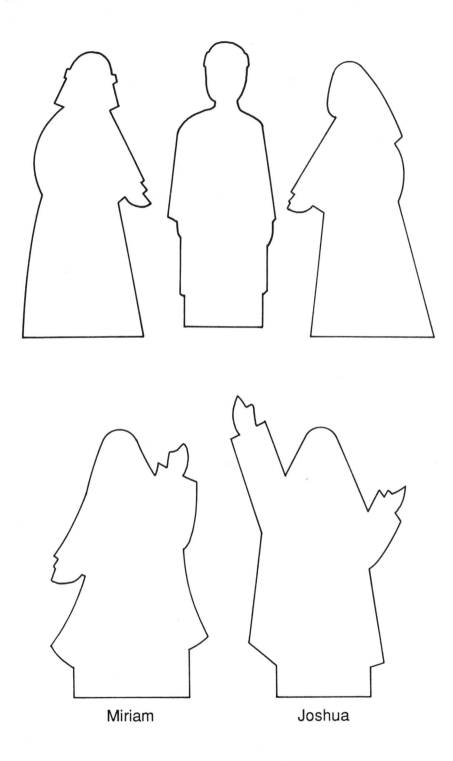

Miriam

Joshua

People of God

Session 10
(also for Sessions 11, 13, and 15)

People of God

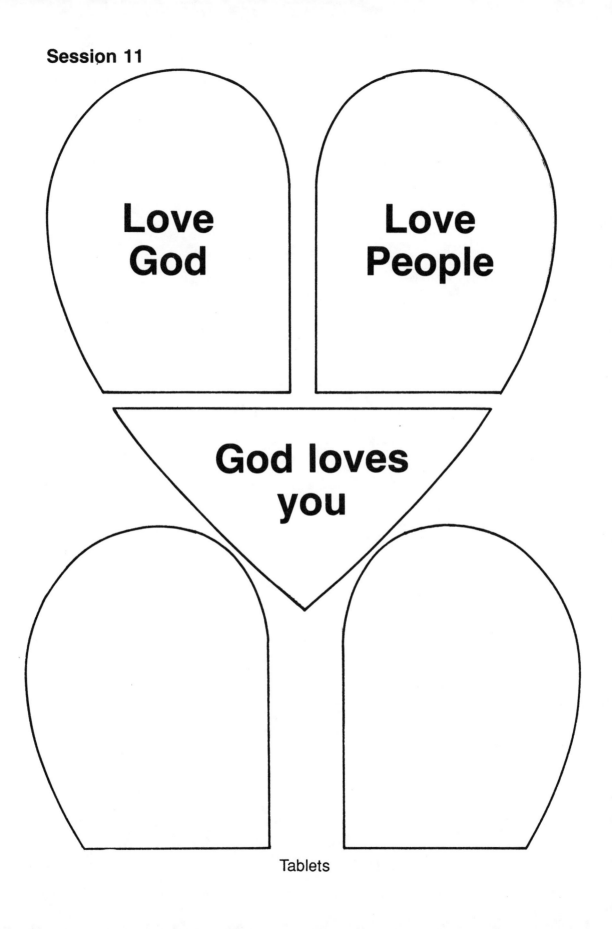

Love God

Love People

God loves you

Tablets

Session 12

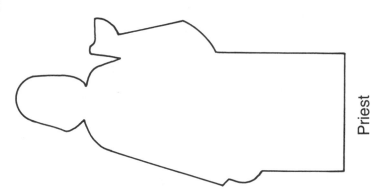

Priest

Session 16

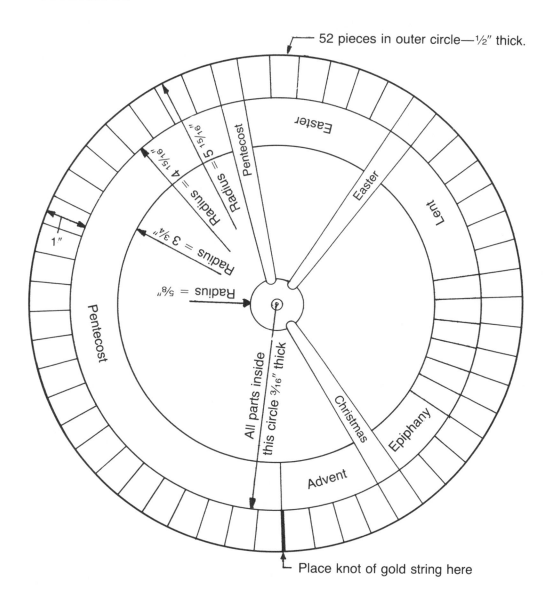

52 pieces in outer circle—½" thick.

Easter

Pentecost

Easter

Lent

Radius = 5 15/16"

Radius = 4 15/16"

Radius = 3 3/4"

Radius = 5/8"

1"

Pentecost

All parts inside this circle 3/16" thick

Christmas

Epiphany

Advent

Place knot of gold string here

Session 13

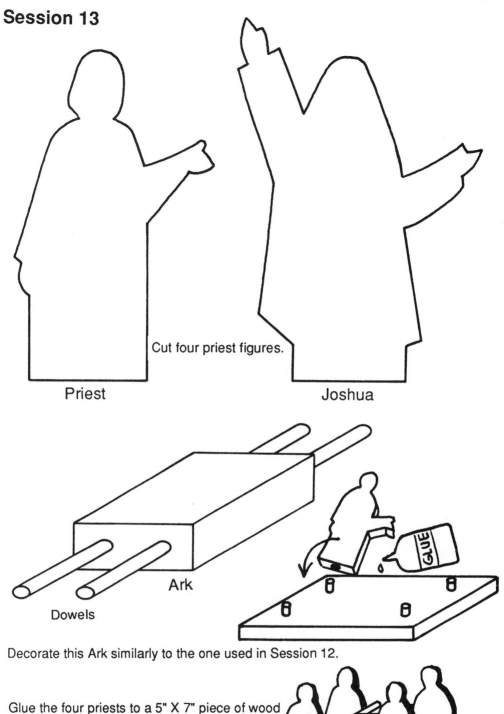

Cut four priest figures.

Priest

Joshua

Ark

Dowels

Decorate this Ark similarly to the one used in Session 12.

Glue the four priests to a 5" X 7" piece of wood
so they can "carry" the Ark more easily.
Use 1/2" pieces of 1/4" dowel to make
a strong joint (see illustration).

Session 16

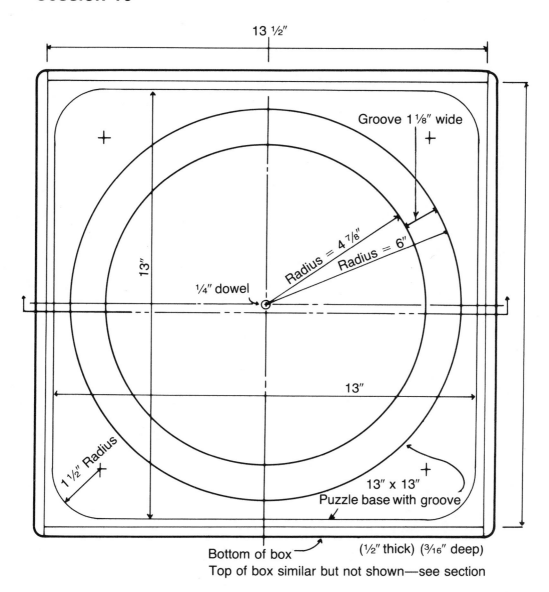

13 ½"

Groove 1 ⅛" wide

+   +

13"

Radius = 4 ⅞"

Radius = 6"

¼" dowel

13"

1 ½" Radius   +

+

13" x 13"
Puzzle base with groove

Bottom of box   (½" thick) (³⁄₁₆" deep)
Top of box similar but not shown—see section

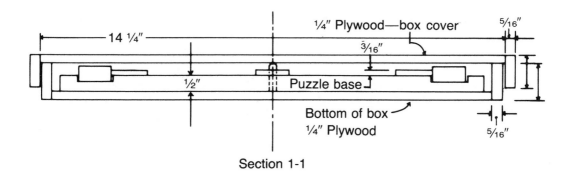

14 ¼"

¼" Plywood—box cover

5⁄16"

³⁄₁₆"

½"

Puzzle base

Bottom of box
¼" Plywood

5⁄16"

Section 1-1

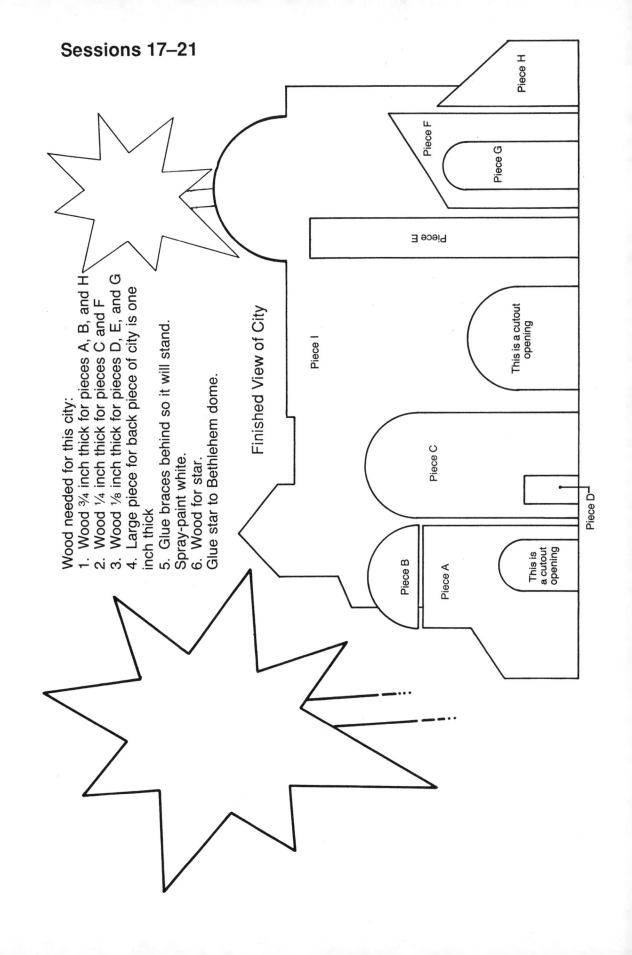

Wood needed for this city:
1. Wood ¾ inch thick for pieces A, B, and H
2. Wood ¼ inch thick for pieces C and F
3. Wood ⅛ inch thick for pieces D, E, and G
4. Large piece for back piece of city is one inch thick
5. Glue braces behind so it will stand. Spray-paint white.
6. Wood for star.
Glue star to Bethlehem dome.

Finished View of City

Piece I

Piece H

Piece F

Piece G

Piece E

This is a cutout opening

Piece C

Piece D

Piece B

Piece A

This is a cutout opening

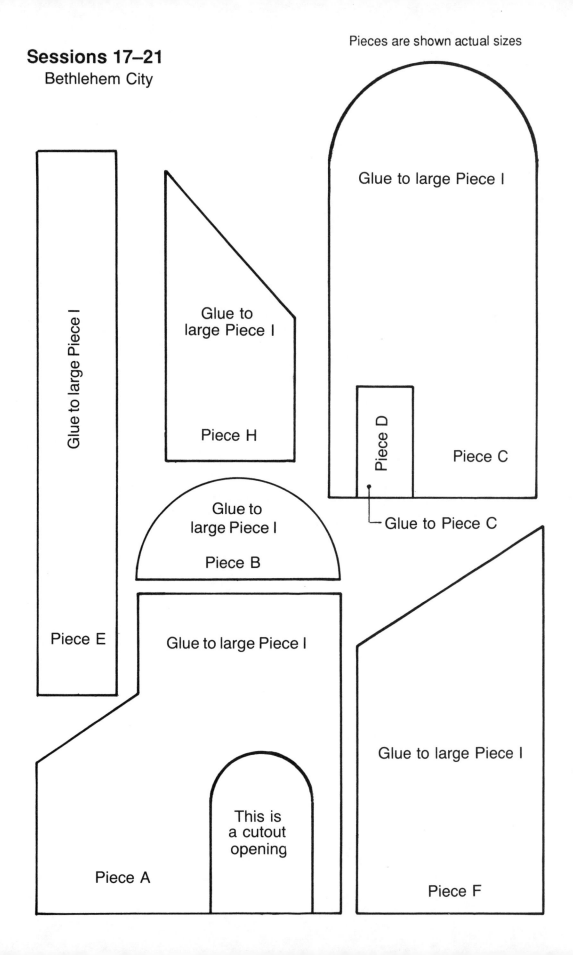

Sessions 17–21
Bethlehem City

Pieces are shown actual sizes

Glue to large Piece I

Glue to large Piece I

Glue to
large Piece I

Piece H

Piece D

Piece C

Glue to large Piece I

Glue to
large Piece I

Piece B

Glue to Piece C

Piece E

Glue to large Piece I

Glue to large Piece I

This is
a cutout
opening

Piece A

Piece F

Sessions 17–21

Enlarge Piece I to 10³/4" X 7¹/2". Piece G is shown actual size.

Glue to
Piece F

Piece G

Piece I

2³/8" 2"

Bethlehem City

Sessions 17–21

Use these patterns both for wooden Nativity figures and Advent card figures.

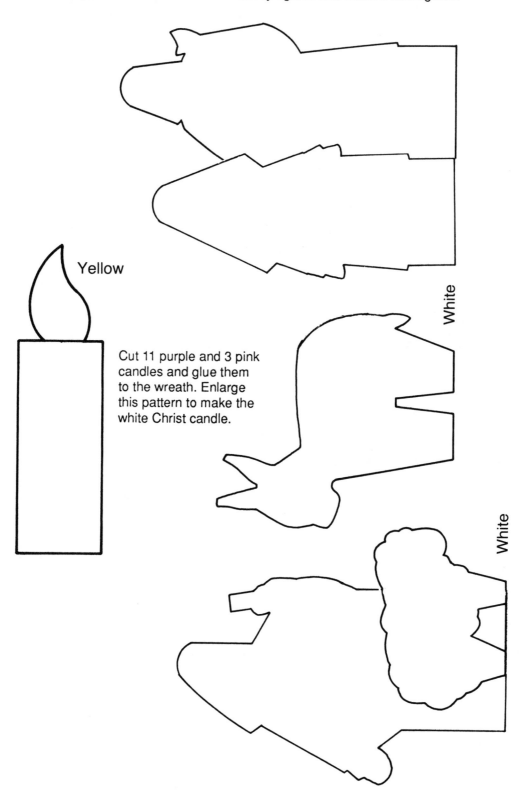

Yellow

Cut 11 purple and 3 pink candles and glue them to the wreath. Enlarge this pattern to make the white Christ candle.

White

White

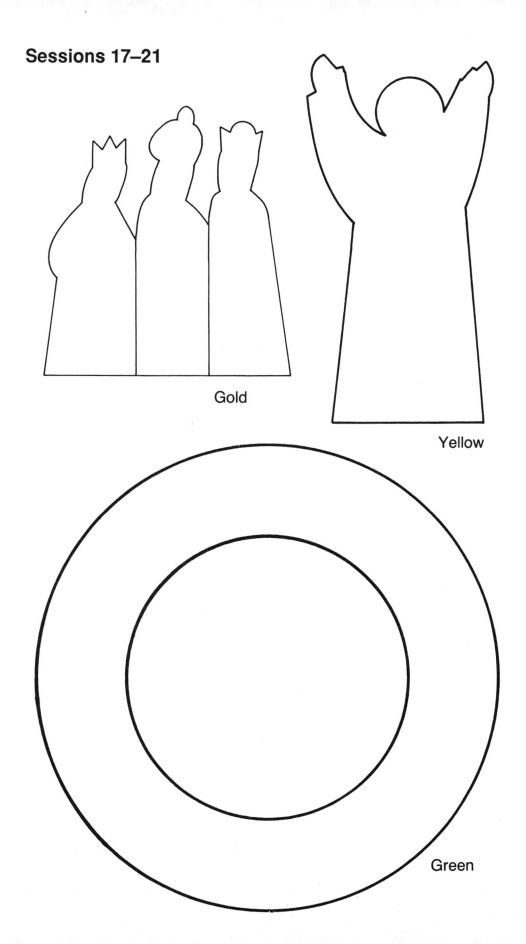

Gold

Yellow

Green

Use the patterns on this page to make wooden Nativity figures.

Christ child in manger

Camel

Session 22

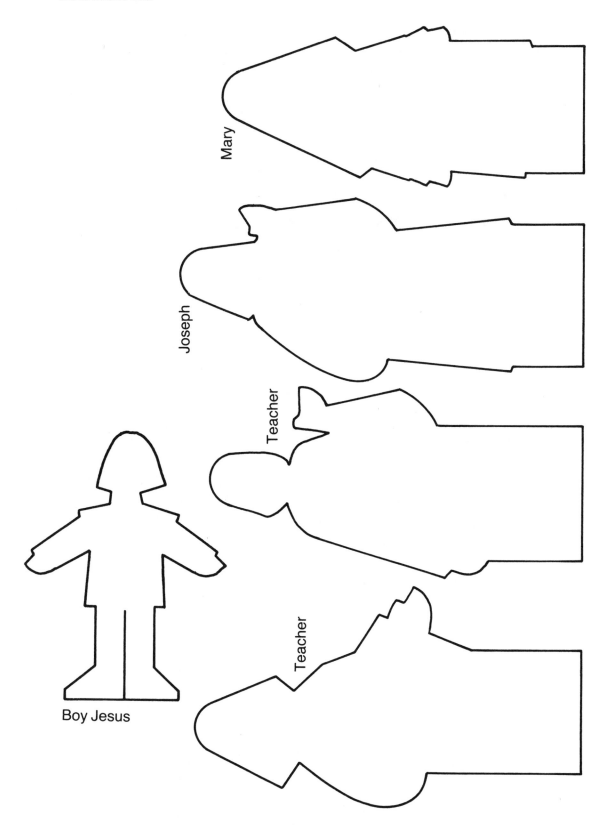

Mary

Joseph

Teacher

Teacher

Boy Jesus

Session 22

Finished size:

Larger base: 7 inches by 9 ¼ inches by ½ inch
Smaller base: 6 inches by 8 inches by ½ inch
Temple: 4 inches by 5 ¾ inches by 6 inches
  pillars: each ½ inch by 5 ½ inches by ¼ inch
  roof line, front and back: 4 inches by ½ inch by ¼ inch
  roof line, sides: 5 ¾ inches by ½ inch by ¼ inch

The temple is a solid piece so glue and clamp smaller pieces to make as above.

Glue and clamp the smaller base to the larger leaving ¾ of an inch from the front and ½ inch on the sides and back.

Glue molding onto temple.

Glue temple onto base leaving 1 ½ inches from the front to the molding (or 1 ¾ inches from the front to the corner of the temple), and 1 inch on both sides, and ½ in the back.

Session 22

Temple for: Sessions 22 and 24

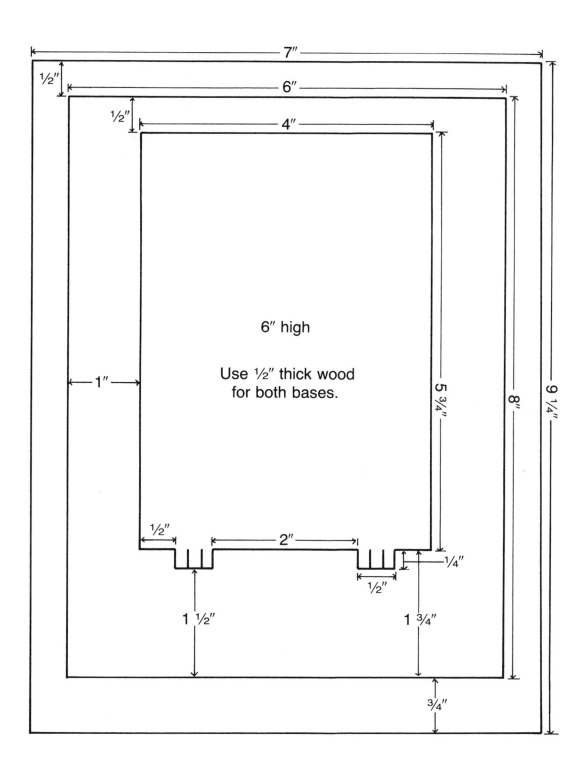

7"

½"

6"

½"

4"

½"

6" high

Use ½" thick wood
for both bases.

1"

5 ¾"

8"

9 ¼"

½"

2"

¼"

½"

1 ½"

1 ¾"

¾"

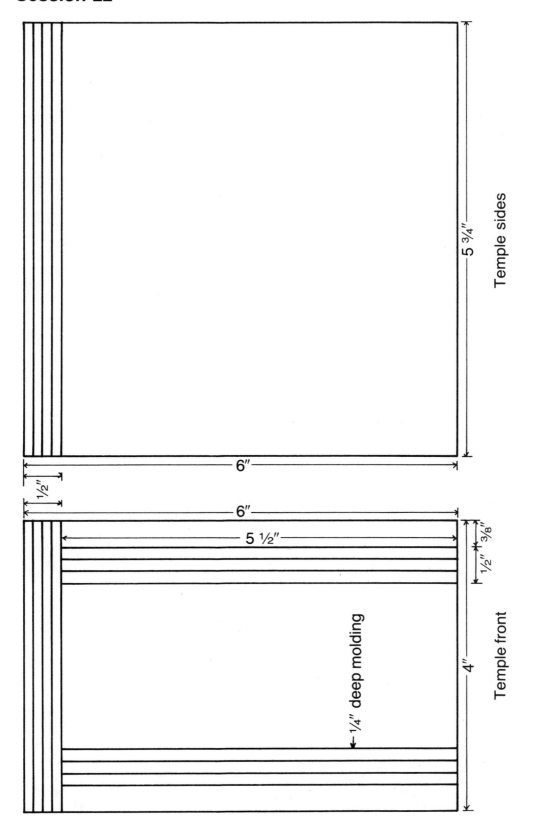

Temple sides

5 ¾"

6"

½"

6"

5 ½"

½" 3/8"

4"

Temple front

¼" deep molding

Session 23

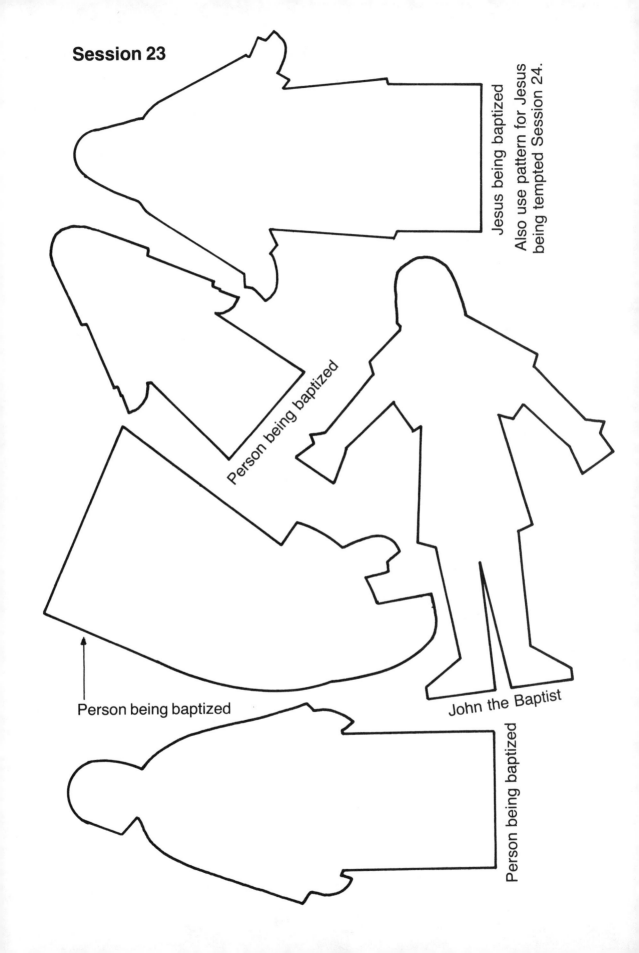

Jesus being baptized

Also use pattern for Jesus being tempted Session 24.

Person being baptized

Person being baptized

John the Baptist

Person being baptized

Session 25

Mustard tree

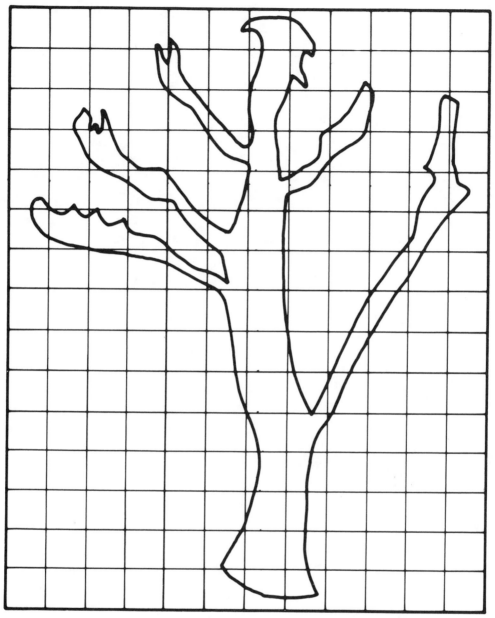

Each square = 2" X 2"

Nests

Session 25

Nests

Birds

Session 26

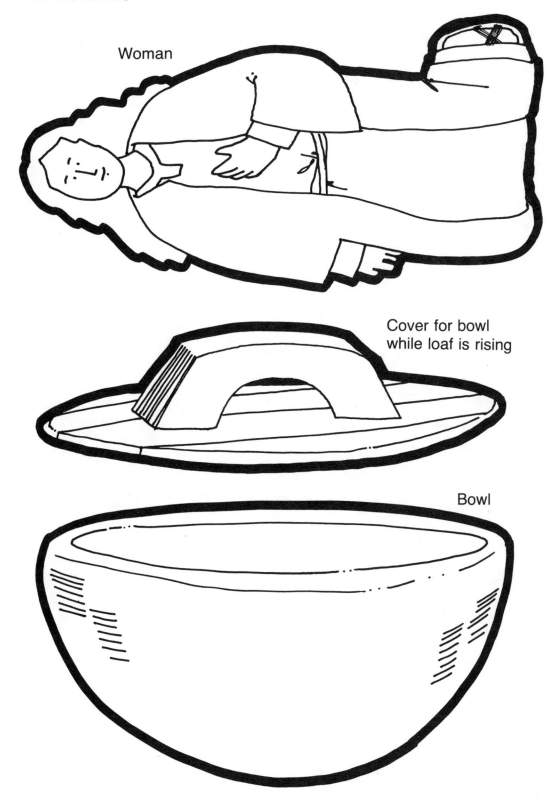

Woman

Cover for bowl
while loaf is rising

Bowl

Session 26

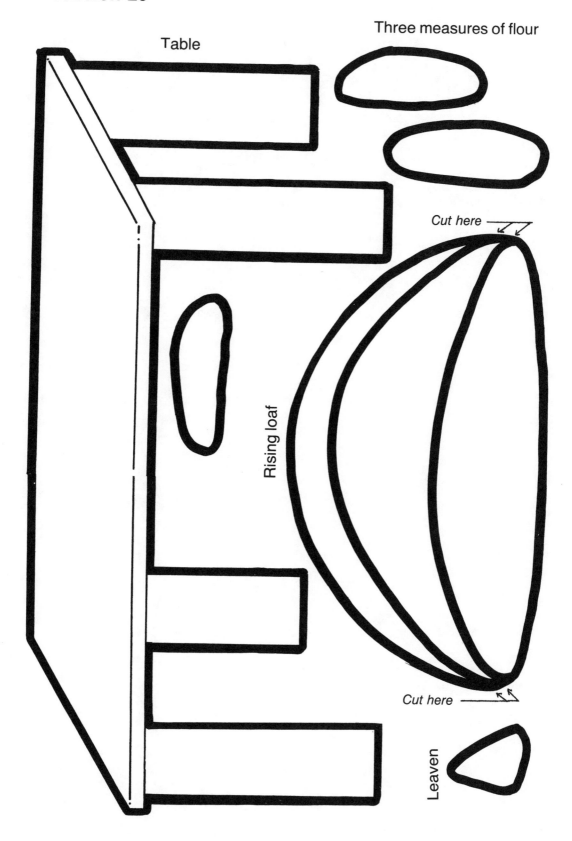

Table

Three measures of flour

Cut here

Rising loaf

Cut here

Leaven

Seller   Merchant

Session 27

Money bags

Flask

Flask is also for use in Session 26

Bed

Table

Lamp

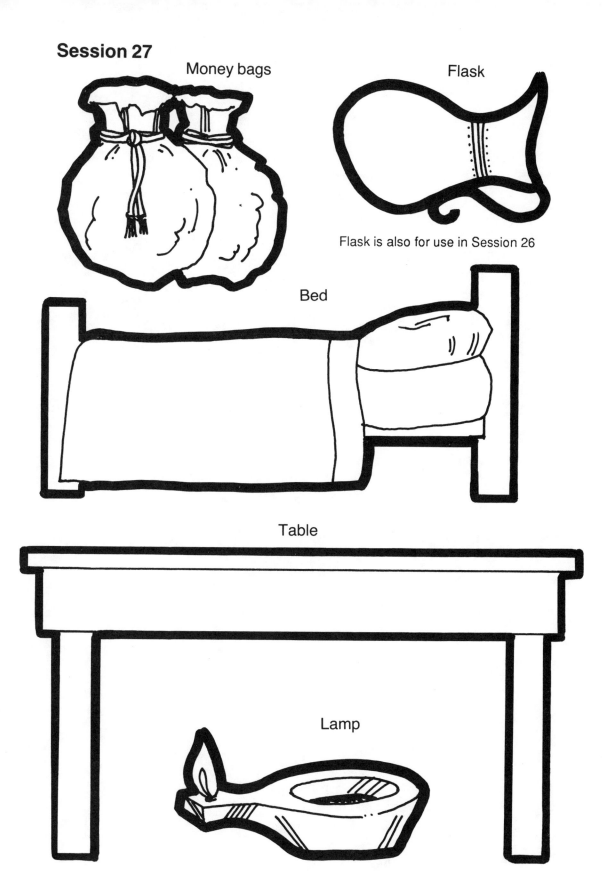

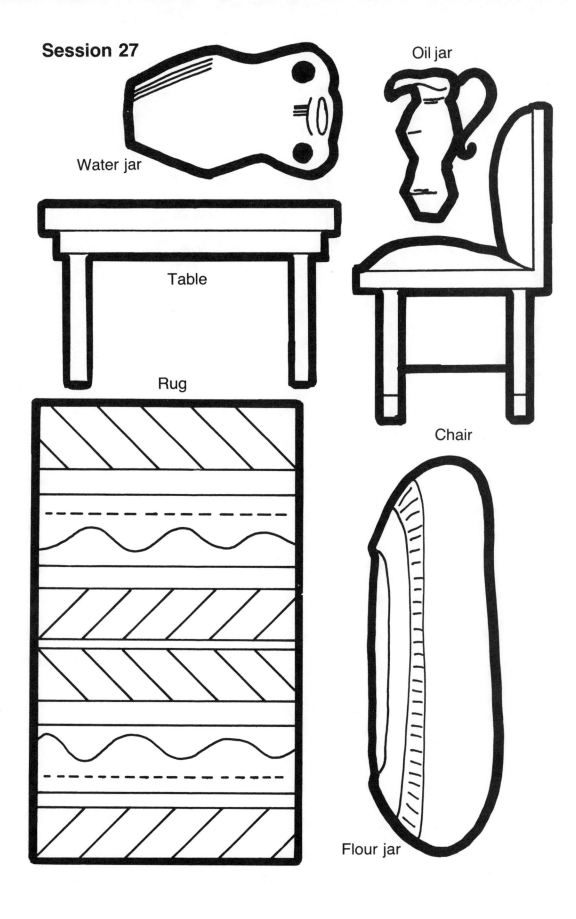

Session 27

Water jar

Oil jar

Table

Chair

Rug

Flour jar

Session 28
Bird pattern piece found in Session 25

30

60

100

Sower

Sacks of grain

Session 28

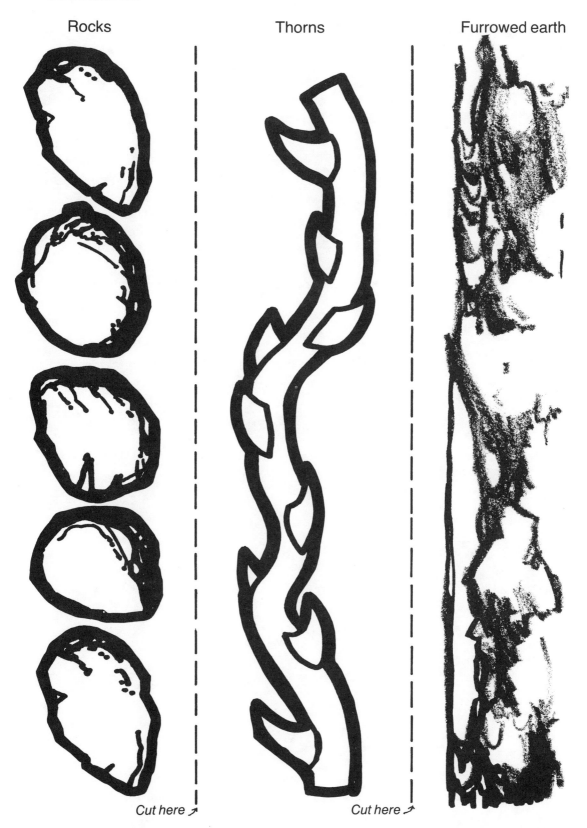

Rocks

Thorns

Furrowed earth

Cut here ↗

Cut here ↗

Robber

Samaritan

Robber

Session 29

Levite

Traveler

Priest

Session 29

City of Jerusalem

City of Jericho

Samaritan and Traveler

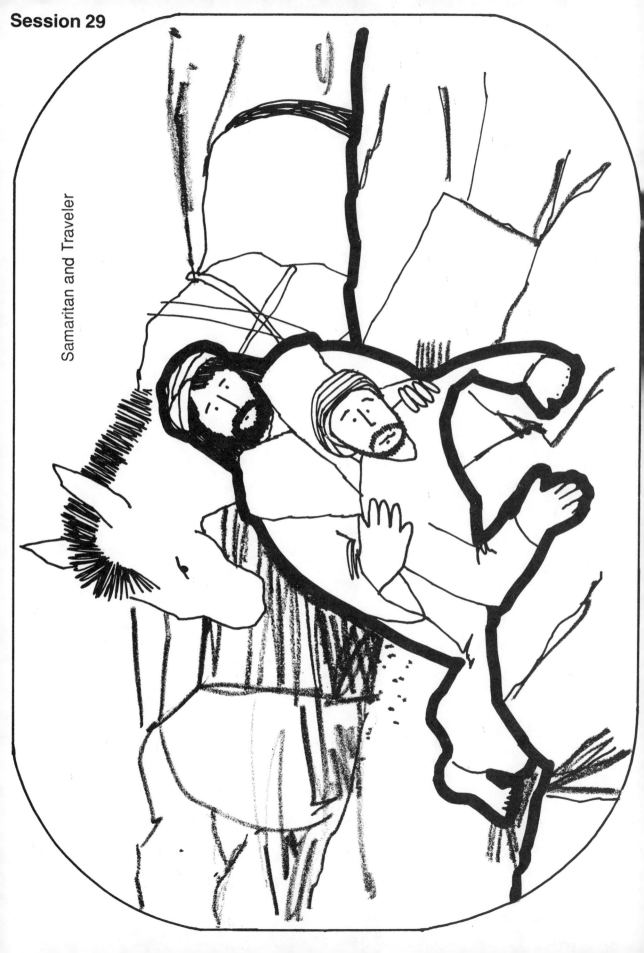

Session 30

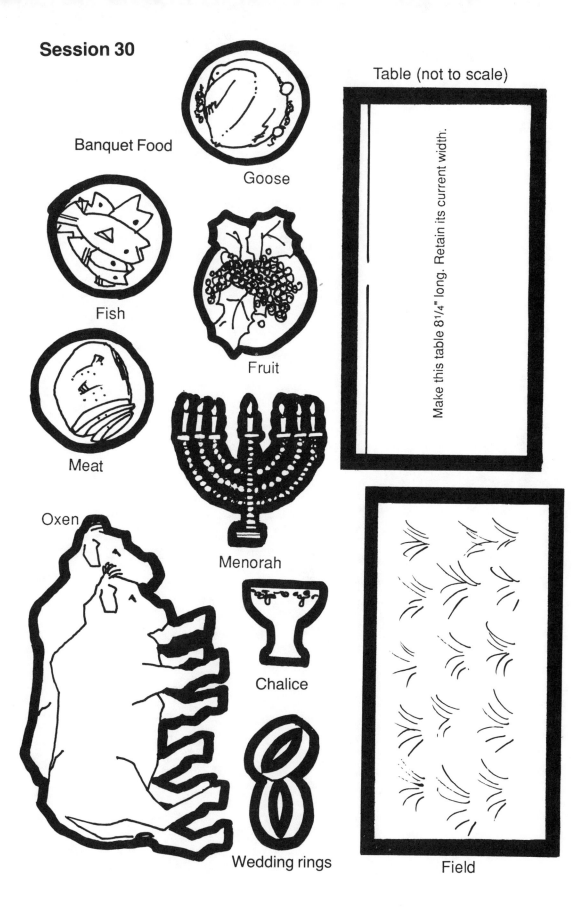

Banquet Food

Goose

Fish

Fruit

Meat

Menorah

Oxen

Chalice

Wedding rings

Table (not to scale)

Make this table 8¼" long. Retain its current width.

Field

Session 30

Bread

Host

Lame

Maimed

Blind

Session 30

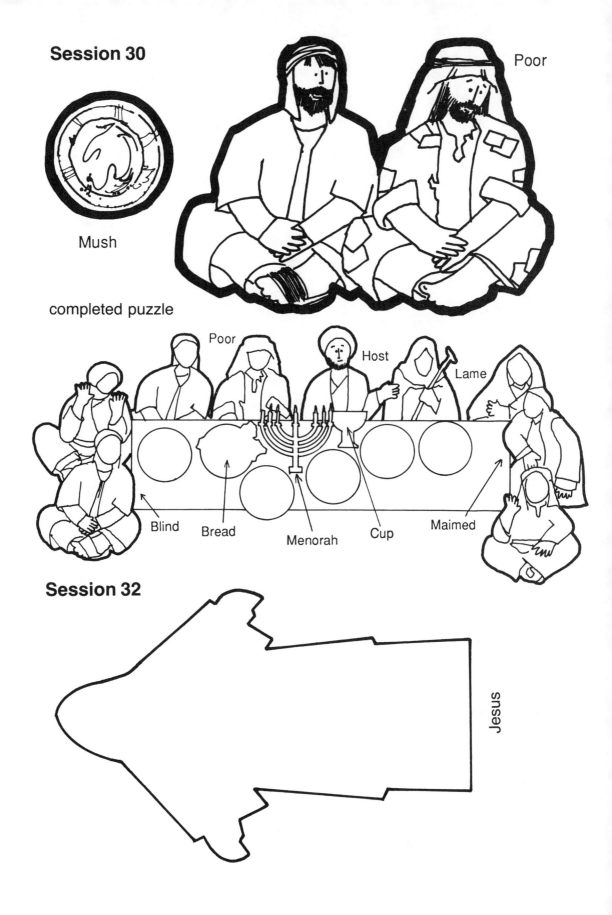

Mush

Poor

completed puzzle

Poor

Host

Lame

Blind

Bread

Menorah

Cup

Maimed

Session 32

Jesus

Session 32

Children

Disciple

Disciple patterns can be
reduced to make figures
for Session 36.

Disciple

Session 32

Model of city of Jerusalem
finished view

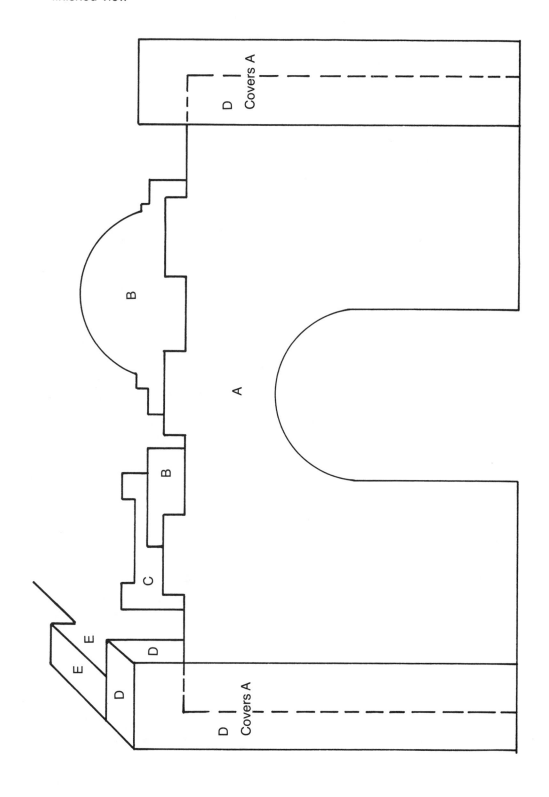

Session 32
Jerusalem
Sections B-D

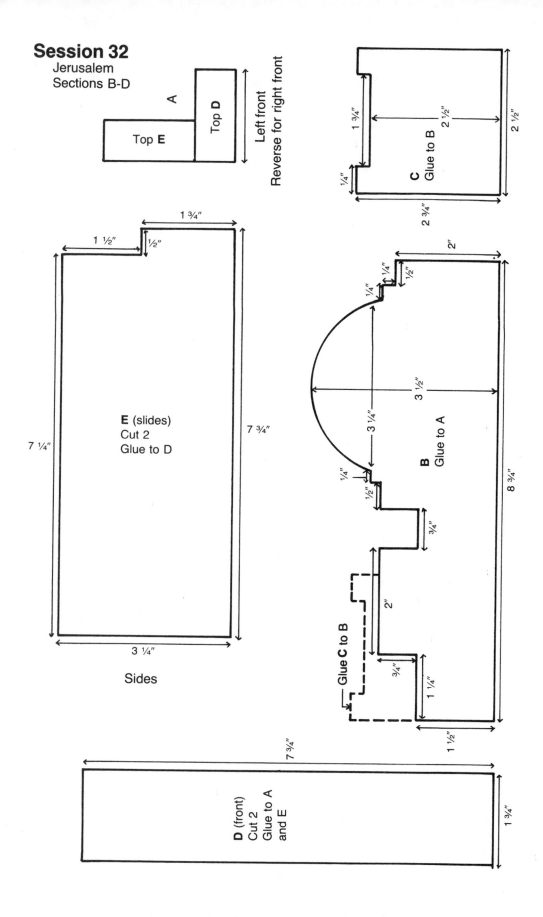

A

Top **D**

Top **E**

Left front
Reverse for right front

1 3/4"
2 1/2"
2 1/2"
C
Glue to B
2 3/4"

1 3/4"
1 1/2"
1/2"
1/4"
1/4"
1/2"
1/4"
2"
1/4"
1/2"
3 1/4"
3 1/2"
B
Glue to A
8 3/4"
3/4"
2"
Glue **C** to B
3/4"
1 1/4"
1 1/2"

7 1/4"
7 3/4"
E (slides)
Cut 2
Glue to D
3 1/4"
Sides

7 3/4"
D (front)
Cut 2
Glue to A
and E
1 3/4"

Session 32

Model of city of Jerusalem

Section A Jerusalem
13″ x 7 ⅛″ x ¾″ (thick)

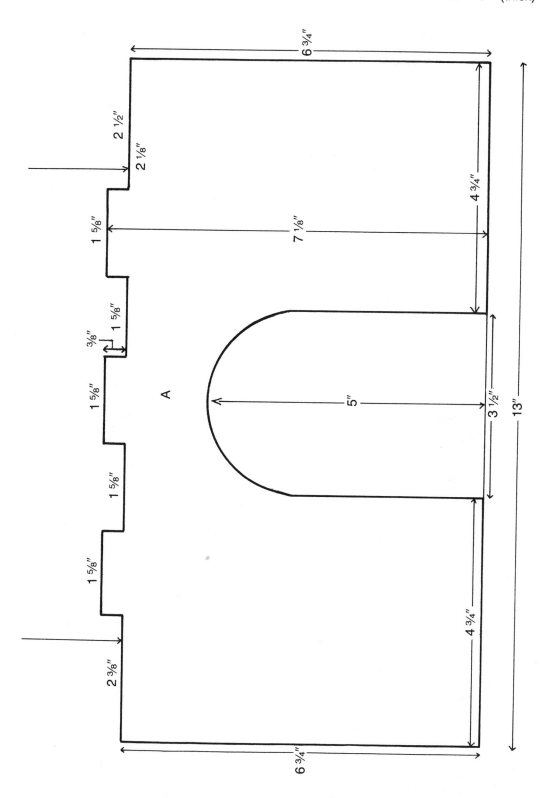

Session 33

Jesus pattern piece found in Session 32
Child pattern piece found in Session 32

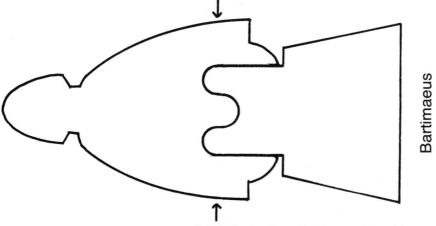

Bartimaeus

Drill hole for dowel before making this cut.

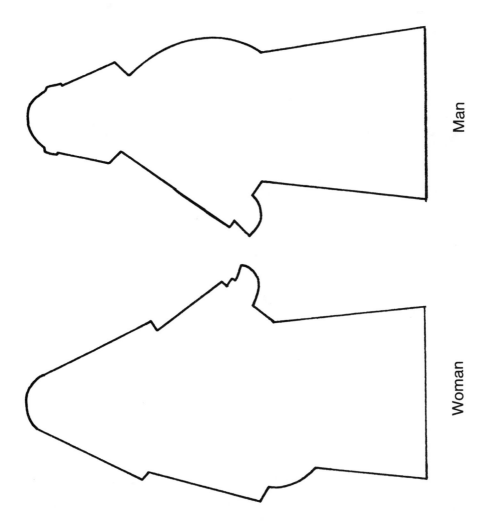

Man

Woman

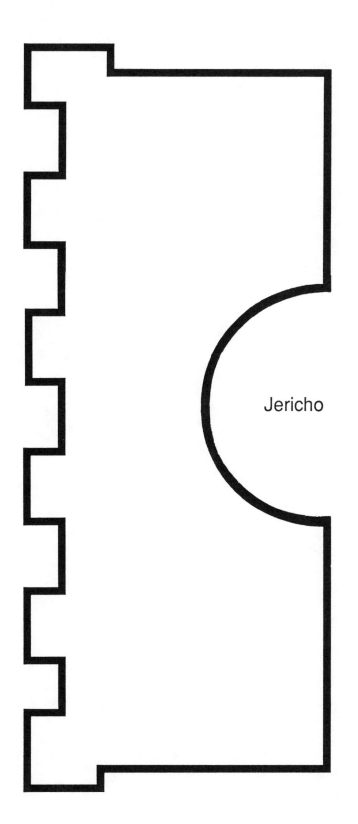

Jericho

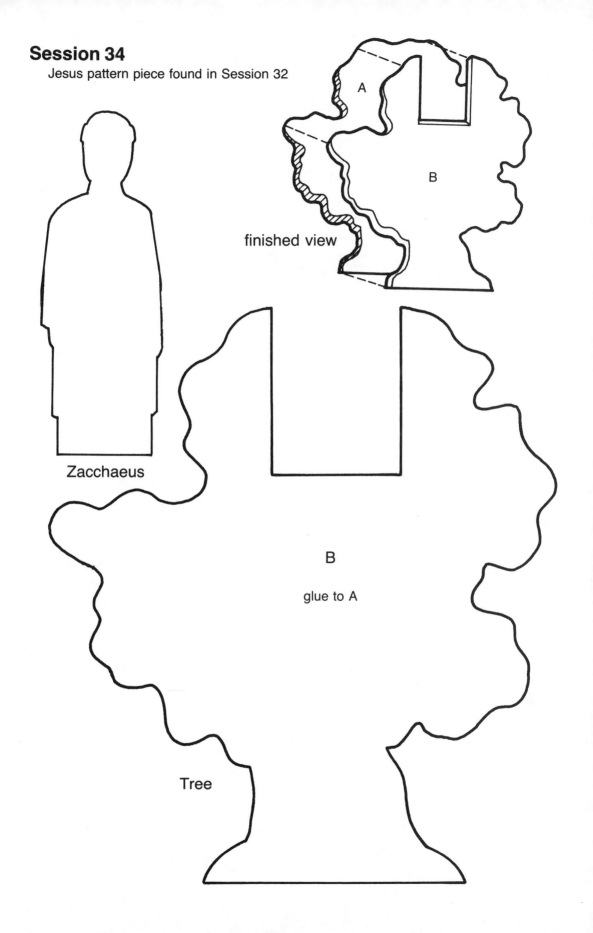

Session 34
Jesus pattern piece found in Session 32

A

B

finished view

Zacchaeus

B

glue to A

Tree

Session 34

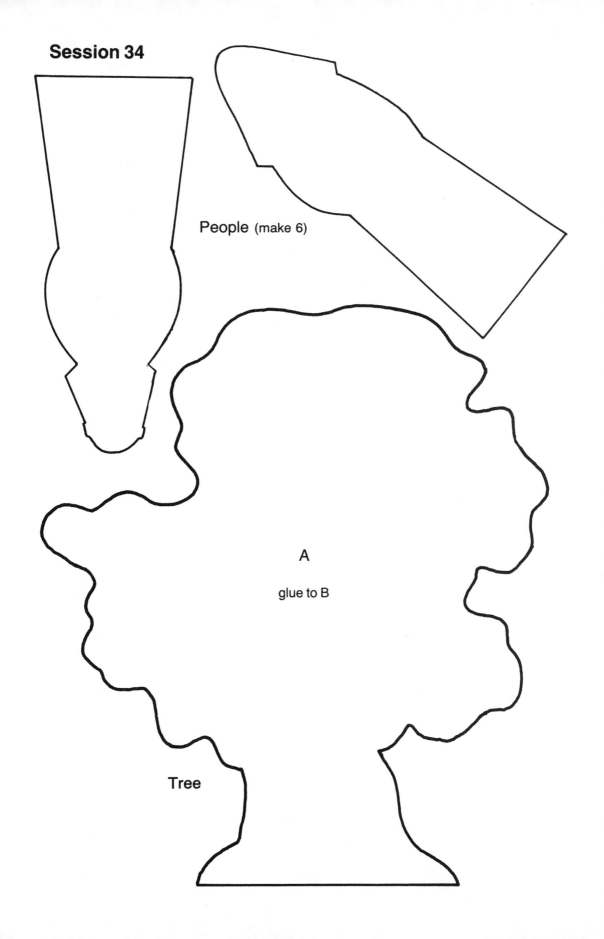

People (make 6)

A

glue to B

Tree

Session 35

Jesus on a donkey

Sessions 36 and 43
Use the Jesus pattern piece found in Session 37.

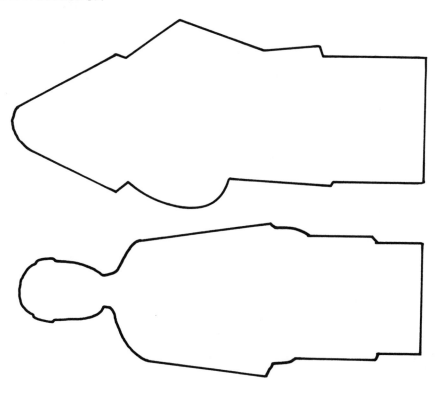

Disciples

For Session 36, cut two each of these disciples and those on the next page for a total of twelve. For Session 43, cut three of these disciples plus two women disciples from the Session 37 patterns.

Sessions 36
and 43
Disciples

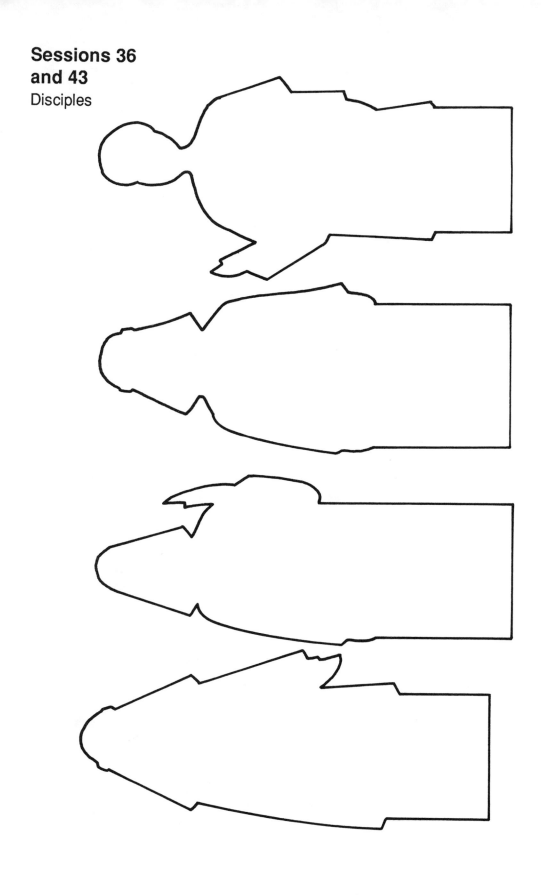

Sessions 36 and 43

Disciples

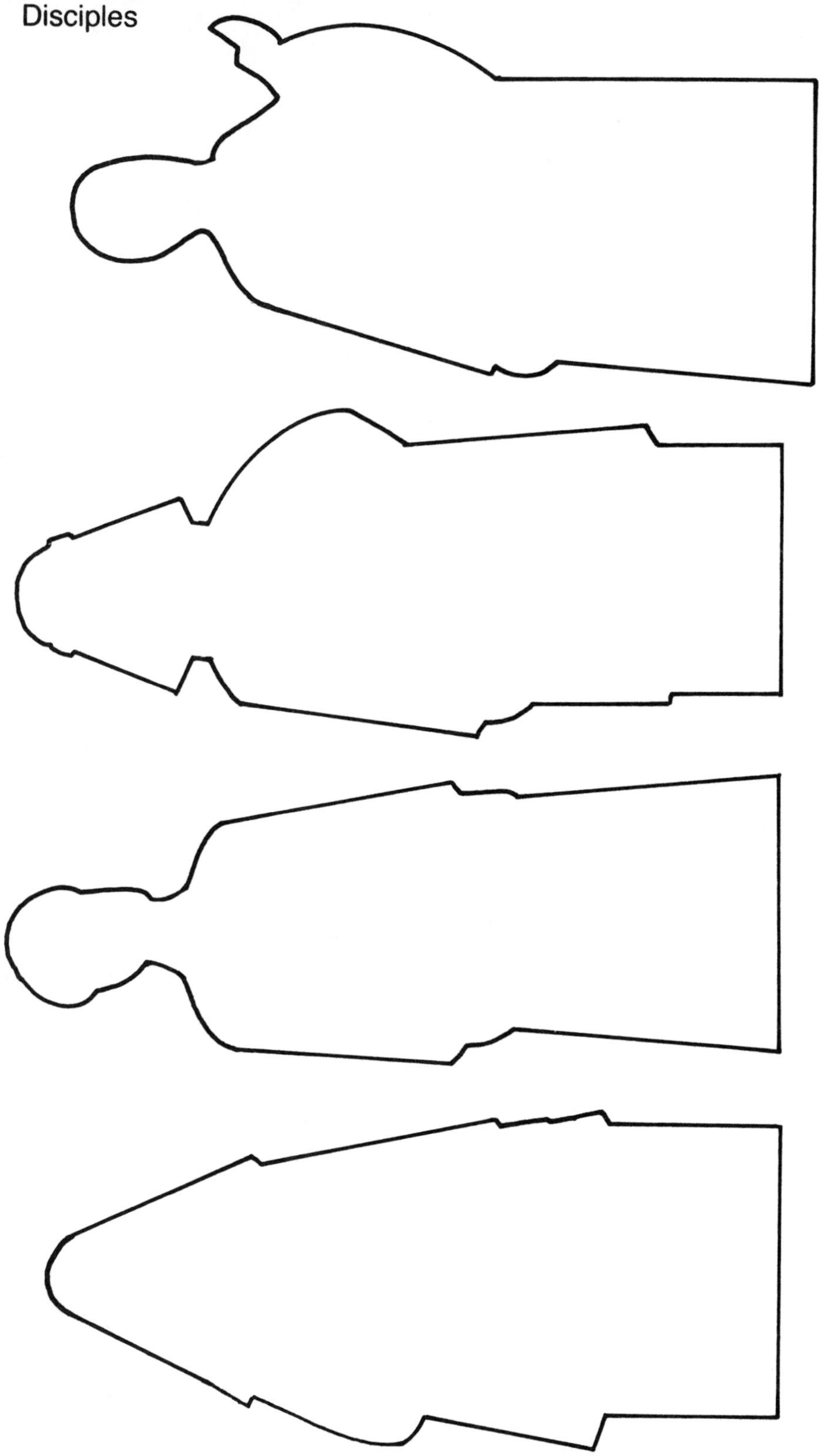

Table
3 ½″ x 8 ½″ x 2″ high

Top

2″ high

Sides
cut 2

**Sessions 37
and 43**

Mary

Use the two patterns for women to make two women disciples for Session 43.

Woman

Woman

Angel

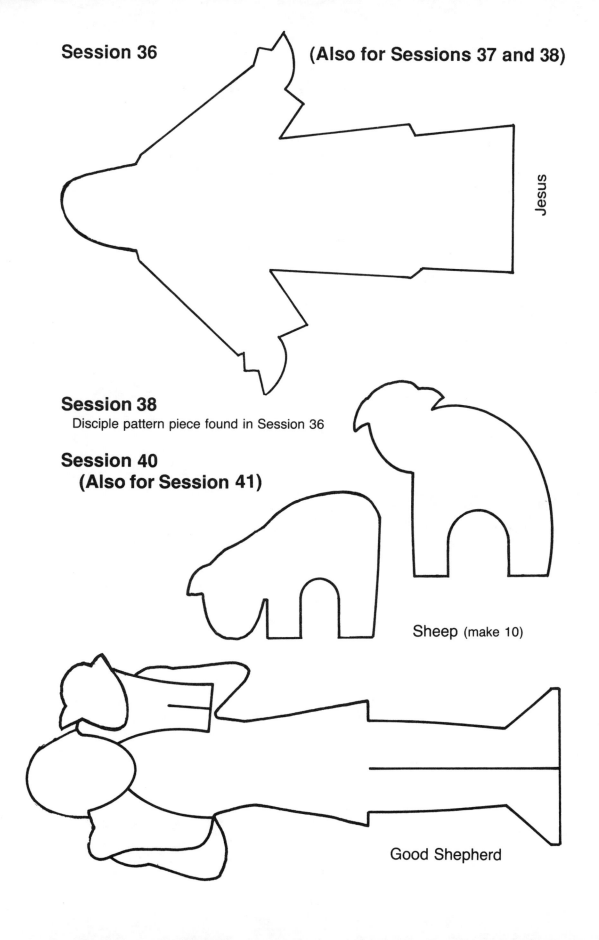

Session 36 (Also for Sessions 37 and 38)

Jesus

Session 38
Disciple pattern piece found in Session 36

Session 40
(Also for Session 41)

Sheep (make 10)

Good Shepherd

Children

Pastor

Session 41

Table pattern piece found in Session 36
For patterns for Session 43, see Sessions 36
and 37 for instructions

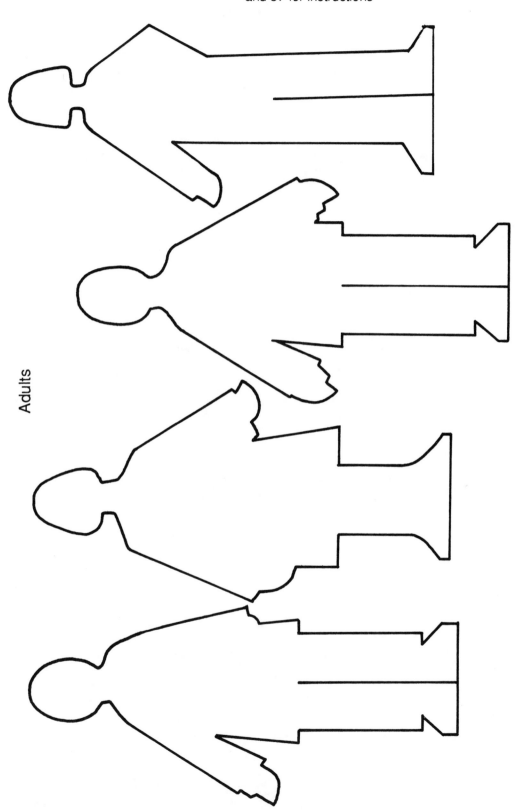

Adults